CW00421715

## Income tax rates (p. 1)

|  | 2003–04 | 2002–03 |  |
|---|---|---|---|
|  | % | % | % |
| Starting rate | 10 | 10 | 10 |
| Basic rate | 22 | 22 | 22 |
| Higher rate | 40 | 40 | 40 |
| Rate on non-dividend savings income | 10/20/40[1] | 10/20/40[1] | 10/20/40[1] |
| Rate on dividend income | 10/32.5[1] | 10/32.5[1] | 10/32.5[1] |
| Rate applicable to trusts | 34[2] | 34 | 34 |
| Schedule F trust rate | 25[2] | 25 | 25 |
|  | £ | £ | £ |
| Starting rate band | 1–1,960 | 1–1,920 | 1–1,880 |
| Basic rate band | 1,961–30,500 | 1,921–29,900 | 1,881–29,400 |

**Notes**

[1] The rate of tax on non-dividend savings income is 10% for starting rate taxpayers, 20% for basic rate taxpayers, and 40% for higher rate taxpayers. The rate of tax on dividend income is 10%, and 32.5% at the higher rate.
[2] The 2003 Pre-Budget Report announced that for 2004–05 the rate applicable to trusts will increase to 40% and the Schedule F rate will increase to 32.5%.

## Taxation of companies (p. 49)

| Financial year | 2003 | 2002 | 2001 |
|---|---|---|---|
| Main rate | 30% | 30% | 30% |
| SC rate[1] | 19% | 19% | 20% |
| Profit limit for SC rate | £300,000 | £300,000 | £300,000 |
| Starting rate[1] | 0% | 0% | 10% |
| Profit limit for starting rate | £10,000 | £10,000 | £10,000 |
| Profit limit for starting rate marginal relief | £50,000 | £50,000 | £50,000 |
| Marginal relief fraction | 19/400 | 19/400 | 1/40 |
| Small company relief fraction | 11/400 | 11/400 | 1/40 |

**Note**

[1] The starting rate and small companies' rate are not available to 'close investment-holding companies'.

## Taxation of capital gains (p. 93)

| Exemptions and reliefs | 2004–05 | 2003–04 | 2002–03 | 2001–02 |
|---|---|---|---|---|
|  | £ | £ | £ | £ |
| Annual exempt amount | 8,200 | 7,900 | 7,700 | 7,500 |
| Chattel exemption (max. sale proceeds) | 6,000 | 6,000 | 6,000 | 6,000 |
| Maximum retirement relief | _[1] | _[1] | 125,000 | 250,000 |

**Note**

[1] Retirement relief ceases to be available from 6 April 2003.

## Inheritance tax (p. 107)

| | Gross rate of tax | |
|---|---|---|
| | Transfers on death | Lifetime transfers |
| Gross cumulative transfer (on or after 6 April 2003)<br>£ | % | % |
| 1–255,000 | Nil | Nil |
| 255,000 upwards | 40 | 20 |

**Note**

Estate on death taxed as top slice of cumulative transfers in the seven years before death. Most lifetime transfers (other than to discretionary trusts) are potentially exempt, only becoming chargeable where death occurs within seven years.

| | |
|---|---|
| Annual exemption | £3,000 |
| Small gift exemption | £250 |

**Note**

[1] The inheritance tax threshold is £263,000 from 6 April 2004.

## VAT (p. 123)

| | |
|---|---|
| Standard rate | 17.5% |
| Annual registration limit – taxable supplies (from 25 April 2003) | £56,000 |
| De-registration limit – taxable supplies (from 25 April 2003) | £54,000 |
| VAT fraction | 7/47 |

## Insurance premium tax (p. 139)

| | Standard rate | Higher rate |
|---|---|---|
| From 1 July 1999 | 5% | 17.5% |
| From 1 April 1997 to 30 June 1999 | 4% | 17.5% |

## Landfill tax (p. 140)

| Period | Lower rate (inert waste)<br>£<br>per tonne | Standard rate<br>£<br>per tonne |
|---|---|---|
| 1 April 2004–31 March 2005 | 2 | 15 |
| 1 April 2003–31 March 2004 | 2 | 14 |
| 1 April 2002–31 March 2003 | 2 | 13 |
| 1 April 2001–31 March 2002 | 2 | 12 |
| 1 April 2000–31 March 2001 | 2 | 11 |
| 1 April 1999–31 March 2000 | 2 | 10 |
| 1 October 1996–31 March 1999 | 2 | 7 |

## Aggregates levy (p. 141)

| Period of application | Rate (per tonne)<br>£ |
|---|---|
| From 1 April 2002 | 1.60 |

## National Insurance contributions (p. 45)

| Class 1 primary (employee) contributions | 2004–05 | 2003–04 | 2002–03 |
|---|---|---|---|
| Lower earnings limit (LEL) | £79 weekly | £77 weekly | £75 weekly |
| Primary threshold | £91 weekly | £89 weekly | £89 weekly |
| Rate up to primary threshold | 0% | 0% | 0% |
| Rate between primary threshold and UEL (not contracted-out) | 11% | 11% | 10% |
| Rate above UEL | 1% | 1% | – |
| Rate between primary threshold and UEL (contracted-out) | 9.4% | 9.4% | 8.4% |
| Reduced rate | 4.85% (£91.01–£610); 1% above £610 | 4.85% (£89.01–£595); 1% above £595 | 3.85% |
| Upper earnings limit (UEL) | £610 weekly | £595 weekly | £585 weekly |

| Class 1 secondary (employer) contributions 2003–04 | |
|---|---|
| Secondary threshold | £89 weekly[1] |
| Rates (not contracted-out) | 12.8% above secondary threshold[2] |
| Rates (contracted-out) | 9.3% for salary-related and 11.8% for money-purchase schemes (including 3.5% and 1.0% rebates for earnings from LEL to secondary threshold), then 12.8% above UEL.[3] |

| Class 2 – Self-employed | 2004–05 | 2003–04 | 2002–03 | 2001–02 |
|---|---|---|---|---|
| | £ | £ | £ | £ |
| Small earnings exemption limit (annual) | 4,215 | 4,095 | 4,025 | 3,955 |
| Weekly rate | 2.05 | 2.00 | 2.00 | 2.00 |
| **Class 3 – Voluntary contributions** | **2004–05** | **2003–04** | **2002–03** | **2001–02** |
| | £ | £ | £ | £ |
| Weekly rate | 7.15 | 6.95 | 6.85 | 6.75 |
| **Class 4 – Self-employed** | **2004–05** | **2003–04** | **2002–03** | **2001–02** |
| | £ | £ | £ | £ |
| Annual earnings limit – upper | 31,720 | 30,940 | 30,420 | 29,900 |
| – lower | 4,745 | 4,615 | 4,615 | 4,535 |
| Maximum contributions | — | — | 1,806.35 | 1,775.55 |
| Rate | 8% (£4,745–£31,720); 1% above £31,720 | 8% (£4,615–£30,940); 1% above £30,940 | 7% | 7% |

**Notes**

[1] £91 weekly for 2004–05.
[2] 12.8% above secondary threshold for 2004–05.
[3] For 2004–05, 9.3% for salary-related and 11.8% for money-purchase schemes (including 3.5% and 1.0% rebates for earnings from LEL to secondary threshold), then 12.8% above UEL.

# PREFACE

**Now in its 21st edition,** *Hardman's Tax Rates & Tables* contains the numerical and factual data in everyday use by the tax practitioner. The material is conveniently arranged in eleven sections: income tax, National Insurance contributions, taxation of companies, general, taxation of capital gains tax, inheritance tax, stamp duties, value added tax, insurance premium tax, landfill tax, and aggregates levy.

The book contains the latest available data at the time of going to press. It takes full account of the measures announced in the *Finance Act* 2003 and also the Pre-Budget Report 2003. The data for 2004–05 may be affected by amendments made in the Finance Bill 2004 during its passage through Parliament.

Every effort has been taken to include, within the constraints of available space, the information of greatest use to the practitioner. A number of changes have been made in the light of suggestions received from users of previous years' editions. CCH welcomes further suggestions as to material which might be inserted in future editions.

January 2004

**Note:** The late Philip Hardman was the original editor of *Hardman's Tax Rates & Tables*. CCH gratefully acknowledges the considerable help and guidance that he provided.

## Disclaimer

This publication is sold on the understanding that the publisher is not engaged in rendering legal or accounting advice or other professional services. The publisher, its editors and any authors, consultants or general editors expressly disclaim all and any liability and responsibility to any person, whether a purchaser or reader of this publication or not, in respect of anything and of the consequences of anything, done or omitted to be done by any such person in reliance, whether wholly or partially, upon the whole or any part of the contents of this publication. While this publication is intended to provide accurate information in regard to the subject matter covered, readers entering into transactions on the basis of such information should seek the services of a competent professional adviser.

## Legislative and other material

While copyright in all statutory and other materials resides in the Crown or other relevant body, copyright in the remaining material in this publication is vested in the publisher.

The publisher advises that any statutory or other materials issued by the Crown or other relevant bodies and reproduced or quoted in this publication are not the authorised official versions of those statutory or other materials. In their preparation, however, the greatest care has been taken to ensure exact conformity with the law as enacted or other material as issued.

Crown copyright legislation is reproduced under the terms of Crown Copyright Policy Guidance issued by HMSO. Other Crown Copyright material is reproduced with the permission of the Controller of HMSO. European Communities Copyright material is reproduced with permission.

## Ownership of Trade Marks

The trade mark  is the property of

Commerce Clearing House Incorporated, Riverwoods, Illinois, USA.
(**CCH** INCORPORATED)

ISBN 0 86325 595 7
CCH Code 5543C

© **2004 Wolters Kluwer (UK) Limited**

All rights reserved. No part of this work covered by the publisher's copyright may be reproduced or copied in any form or by any means (graphic, electronic or mechanical, including photocopying, recording, recording taping, or other information and retrieval systems) without the written permission of the publisher.

Typeset in the UK by MFK Mendip.
Printed in the UK by Chiltern Press Ltd.

# ABOUT THE PUBLISHER

Wolters Kluwer (UK) Limited is part of the international Wolters Kluwer Group. Wolters Kluwer is the leading publisher specialising in tax, business and law publishing throughout Europe, the US and the Asia Pacific region. The group produces a wide range of information services in different media for the accounting and legal professions and for business.

All CCH publications are designed to be practical and authoritative reference works and guides and are written by our own highly qualified and experienced editorial team and specialist outside authors.

CCH publishes information packages including electronic products, loose-leaf reporting services, newsletters and books on UK and European legal topics for distribution world-wide. The UK operation also acts as distributor of the publications of the overseas affiliates.

CCH
145 London Road
Kingston-upon-Thames
Surrey
KT2 6SR
Telephone: 0870 777 2906
Facsimile: 0208 247 1184

Part of the Wolters Kluwer Group

# ACKNOWLEDGEMENTS

Certain material in this publication is Crown copyright and is reproduced with the kind permission of the Controller of Her Majesty's Stationery Office.

CCH kindly acknowledges the endorsement of this publication by the Chartered Institute of Taxation and the Tax Faculty of the Institute of Chartered Accountants in England and Wales.

THE CHARTERED INSTITUTE
OF
TAXATION

# INCOME TAX

## Income tax rates 1999–2000 to 2003–04

| | 2003–04 Taxable income £ | Tax £ | 2002–03 Taxable income £ | Tax £ | 2001–02 Taxable income £ | Tax £ | 2000–01 Taxable income £ | Tax £ | 1999–2000 Taxable income £ | Tax £ |
|---|---|---|---|---|---|---|---|---|---|---|
| Starting rate | 1,960 @ 10% = | 196.00 | 1,920 @ 10% = | 192.00 | 1,880 @ 10% = | 188.00 | 1,520 @ 10% = | 152.00 | 1,500 @ 10% = | 150.00 |
| Basic rate | 1,961 – 30,500 @ 22% = | 6,278.80 | 1,921 – 29,900 @ 22% = | 6,155.60 | 1,881 – 29,400 @ 22% = | 6,054.40 | 1,521 – 28,400 @ 22% = | 5,913.60 | 1,501 – 28,000 @ 23% = | 6,095.00 |
| Higher rate | over 30,500 @ 40% | | over 29,900 @ 40% | | over 29,400 @ 40% | | over 28,400 @ 40% | | over 28,000 @ 40% | |
| Rate on non-dividend savings income | 10% up to starting rate limit 20% up to basic rate limit 40% thereafter | | | | | | | | | |
| Rate on dividend income | 10% up to basic rate limit 32.5% thereafter | | | | | | | | | |
| Rate applicable to trusts | 34%[1] | | | | | | | | | |
| Schedule F trust rate | 25%[1] | | | | | | | | | |

### Notes

[1] The 2003 Pre-Budget Report announced that for 2004–05 the rate applicable to trusts will increase to 40% and the Schedule F rate will increase to 32.5%.

## Income tax rates 1997–98 to 1998–99

| | 1998–99 Taxable income £ | Tax £ | 1997–98 Taxable income £ | Tax £ |
|---|---|---|---|---|
| Lower rate | 4,300 @ 20% = | 860 | 4,100 @ 20% = | 820 |
| Basic rate | 4,301 – 27,100 @ 23% = | 5,244 | 4,101 – 26,100 @ 23% = | 5,060 |
| Higher rate | over 27,100 @ 40% | | over 26,100 @ 40% | |
| Additional rate (accumulation and discretionary trusts) | flat rate of 34% applicable to trusts | | 10% (rate applicable to trusts 34%) | |

# Personal allowances and reliefs 1998–99 to 2004–05

| Type of relief | 2004–05 £ | 2003–04 £ | 2002–03 £ | 2001–02 £ | 2000–01 £ | 1999–2000 £ | 1998–99 £ |
|---|---|---|---|---|---|---|---|
| **Personal allowance** | | | | | | | |
| Age under 65 | 4,745 | 4,615 | 4,615 | 4,535 | 4,385 | 4,335 | 4,195 |
| Age 65–74 | 6,830 | 6,610 | 6,100 | 5,990 | 5,790 | 5,720 | 5,410 |
| Age 75 & over | 6,950 | 6,720 | 6,370 | 6,260 | 6,050 | 5,980 | 5,600 |
| **Married couple's allowance (MCA)**[1][2] | | | | | | | |
| Age under 65 | — | — | — | — | — | 1,970 | 1,900 |
| Age 65–74 and born before 6 April 1935 | 5,725 | 5,565 | 5,465 | 5,365 | 5,185 | 5,125 | 3,305 |
| Age 75 & over | 5,795 | 5,635 | 5,535 | 5,435 | 5,255 | 5,195 | 3,345 |
| Minimum amount of MCA[3] | 2,210 | 2,150 | 2,110 | 2,070 | 2,000 | — | — |
| Maximum income before abatement of relief for taxpayers aged 65 and over | 18,900 | 18,300 | 17,900 | 17,600 | 17,000 | 16,800 | 16,200 |
| Abatement income ceiling[3] | | | | | | | |
| **Personal** | | | | | | | |
| —Age 65–74 | 23,070 | 22,290 | 20,870 | 20,510 | 19,810 | 19,570 | 18,630 |
| —Age 75 & over | 23,220 | 22,510 | 21,410 | 21,050 | 20,330 | 20,090 | 19,010 |
| **Married** | | | | | | | |
| —Age 65–74 | 30,100 | 29,120 | 27,580 | 27,100 | 26,180 | 25,880 | 21,440 |
| —Age 75 & over | 30,390 | 29,480 | 28,260 | 27,780 | 26,840 | 26,540 | 21,900 |
| **Additional allowance for children**[1] | — | — | — | — | — | 1,970 | 1,900 |
| **Widow's bereavement allowance**[1] | — | — | — | — | 2,000 | 1,970 | 1,900 |
| **Blind person's allowance** | 1,560 | 1,510 | 1,480 | 1,450 | 1,400 | 1,380 | 1,330 |
| **Life assurance relief** (policies issued before 14 March 1984) | 12.5% of premiums | 12.5% of premiums | 12.5% of premiums | 12.5% of premiums | 12.5% of premiums | 12.5% of premiums | 12.5% of premiums |
| **Mortgage interest:** Loan limit[4] | — | — | — | — | — | 30,000 | 30,000 |
| **'Rent-a-room'** Limit[5] | 4,250 | 4,250 | 4,250 | 4,250 | 4,250 | 4,250 | 4,250 |

## Notes

[1] From 6 April 2000, the MCA is withdrawn except where either spouse was born before 6 April 1935.

[2] From 1999–2000 relief for MCA, and other reliefs linked to it, is restricted to 10%. For 1998–99, it is restricted to 15%.

[3] From 6 April 1989 relief is abated by ½ total income over the maximum income limit (previously ⅔ total income over the maximum income limit) subject to the abatement income ceiling. From 6 April 2000, the married couple's allowance cannot be reduced below the minimum amount shown.

[4] Mortgage interest relief on loans for home purchase is withdrawn from 6 April 2000. From the same date relief is also withdrawn for loans made prior to 6 April 1988 for home improvements or the purchase or improvement of homes for a dependent relative (or for the borrower's divorced or separated spouse). Relief continues at 23% for loans to purchase life annuities taken out before 9 March 1999.

[5] Gross annual rents from furnished letting of rooms in only or main residence exempt for owner occupiers up to specified limit. If more than one person is in receipt of income from furnished residential accommodation in the residence, the exempt limit is halved.

# Tax credits

## Working tax credit – maximum rates

| Element | Maximum annual rate (£) | |
|---|---|---|
| | 2003–04 | 2004–05 |
| Basic element | 1,525 | 1,570 |
| Disability element | 2,040 | 2,100 |
| 30-hour element | 620 | 640 |
| Second adult element | 1,500 | 1,545 |
| Lone parent element | 1,500 | 1,545 |
| Severe disability element | 865 | 890 |
| 50-plus element – | | |
| (a) at least 16 hrs but less than 30 hrs per week | 1,045 | 1,075 |
| (b) at least 30 hrs per week | 1,565 | 1,610 |
| Child care element | 70 per cent of: (a) costs up to £135 per week, where the claimant's family includes only one child in respect of whom relevant child care charges are paid; (b) costs up to £200 per week where the claimant's family includes more than one child in respect of whom relevant child care charges are paid. | |

## Child tax credit – maximum rates

| Element | Maximum annual rate (£) | |
|---|---|---|
| | 2003–04 | 2004–05 |
| Individual element – | | |
| for each: | | |
| child | 1,445 | 1,625 |
| disabled child | 3,600 | 3,840 |
| severely disabled child | 4,465 | 4,730 |
| Family element – | | |
| where any child is under one year | 1,090 | 1,090 |
| otherwise | 545 | 545 |

## Reductions in maximum rates 2003–04 and 2004–05

| Reduction | Applied to |
|---|---|
| 37 per cent of income above £5,060 p.a.[1] | 1. The total of all elements of WTC other than the child care element.<br>2. The child care element of WTC.<br>3. The individual element of CTC.<br>4. The family element of CTC – but adjust the reduction figure brought forward by $\times \dfrac{6.67^{(2),(3)}}{37}$ |

**Notes**

[1] If only CTC is claimed, the threshold is £13,480 for 2004–05 (2003–04 £13,230) p.a.

[2] The family element is not reduced unless income is more than £50,000.

[3] Where the rate, or combined rates, of credit would be less than £26 annually, there is no rate of credit.

## Working families' tax credit (WFTC)[1][4]

Amounts shown in £'s per week

| | | 2002–03 | 2001–02 |
|---|---|---|---|
| Basic tax credit | | 62.50 (before 4 June 2002, 60.00) | 59.00 (before 4 June 2001, 54.00) |
| Credit where one earner works at least 30 hours per week | | 11.65 | 11.45 |
| Child tax credits | Up to 16 | 26.45 | 26.00 |
| | 16–18 | 27.20 | 26.75 |
| | Disabled child | 35.50 | 30.00 |
| Enhanced disability tax credit[2] | lone parent/ couple | 16.25 | 16.00 |
| | child | 11.25 | 11.05 |
| Maximum income before taper[3] | | 94.50 | 92.90 |

**Notes**

[1] The WFTC was available to claimants who are in work, who are responsible for a child or young person, whose net household income does not exceed a prescribed limit, and whose savings do not exceed £8,000. WFTC was administered by the Revenue and was paid to employed claimants via their employer. Self-employed people received WFTC direct from the Revenue. Couples were able to choose whether the mother or father receives the WFTC. The WFTC award was calculated by adding the credits together and normally lasted for 26 weeks.

[2] The enhanced disability tax credit is available for people who are in receipt of the highest rate care component of disability living allowance.

[3] The WFTC is withdrawn at the rate of 55p in every £1 by which net household income exceeds the weekly threshold shown.

[4] The WFTC is replaced by the working tax credit and child tax credit (see p. 3) for 2003–04.

## Disabled person's tax credit (DPTC)[1][4]

Amounts shown in £'s per week

| | | 2002–03 | 2001–02 |
|---|---|---|---|
| Basic tax credit | Single person | 62.10 | 61.05 (before 4 June 2001, 56.05) |
| | Couple or lone parent | 95.30 (before 4 June 2002, 92.80) | 91.25 (before 4 June 2001, 86.25) |
| Credit where claimant or partner works at least 30 hours per week | | 11.65 | 11.45 |
| Child tax credits | Up to 16 | 26.45 | 26.00 |
| | 16–18 | 27.20 | 26.75 |
| | Disabled child | 35.50 | 30.00 |
| Enhanced disability tax credit[2] | Single person | 11.25 | 11.05 |
| | lone parent/ couple | 16.25 | 16.00 |
| | child | 11.25 | 11.05 |
| Maximum income before taper[3] | Single person | 73.50 | 72.25 |
| | couple or lone parent | 94.50 | 92.90 |

**Notes**

[1] The DPTC is payable to a claimant with an illness or disability that puts him or her at a disadvantage in getting a job, who receives one of a number of qualifying benefits, whose net household income does not exceed a prescribed amount, and whose savings do not exceed £16,000. It is administered by the Revenue and is paid to employed claimants via their employer.

[2] The enhanced disability tax credit is available to people who are in receipt of the highest rate care component of disability living allowance.

[3] The DPTC is withdrawn by 55p for every £1 by which net household income exceeds the weekly thresholds shown.

[4] The DPTC is replaced by the working tax credit and child tax credit (see p. 3) for 2003–04.

**Childcare tax credit**

| | 2002–03 | 2001–02 |
|---|---|---|
| Childcare tax credit | 70% of eligible childcare costs up to a maximum of:<br>• £135 a week costs for one child (i.e. maximum of £94.50 credit); and<br>• £200 a week costs for more than one (i.e. maximum of £140 credit). | 70% of eligible childcare costs up to a maximum of:<br>**Pre June 2001:**<br>• £100 a week costs for one child (i.e. maximum of £70 credit); and<br>• £150 a week for more than one (i.e. maximum of £105 credit).<br>**From June 2001:**<br>• £135 a week costs for one child (i.e. maximum of £94.50 credit); and<br>• £200 a week costs for more than one (i.e. maximum £140 credit). |

# Submission of personal tax returns: 2003–04

The return must be filed by 31 January 2005, except in the following circumstances:

| Circumstances | Filing date |
|---|---|
| Taxpayer wishes the Revenue to calculate the tax liability in time for first payment date or repayment:<br>• return issued by 31 July 2004 | 30 September 2004 (paper returns); 31 December 2004 (electronically delivered returns) |
| • return issued after 31 July 2004 | Two months from date of issue |
| Taxpayer making self-assessment – return issued after 31 October 2004 | Three months from date of issue |
| Taxpayer wishes underpayment (below £2,000) to be coded out under 2005–06 PAYE (paper returns) | 30 September 2004 |
| Taxpayer wishes underpayment (below £2,000) to be coded out under 2005–06 PAYE (electronically delivered returns) | 31 December 2004 |

# Main penalty provisions

## Individuals: 2003–04

| Offence | Penalty[1][2] |
|---|---|
| Late return (TMA 1970, s. 93)[3][4]: <br>• if return not filed by 1 February 2004 <br>• if return still not filed by 31 July 2005 <br>• if return not filed after 1 February 2006 <br>• for continuing delay on application to the commissioners | £100 <br>£100 <br>Tax geared <br><br>Up to £60 per day |
| Failure to notify chargeability (TMA 1970, s. 7) | Tax geared |
| Incorrect return, accounts and claims made fraudulently or negligently (TMA 1970, s. 95) | Tax geared |
| Failure to keep and retain tax records (TMA 1970, s. 12B) | Up to £3,000 per year of assessment |
| False statements to reduce interim payments (TMA 1970, s. 59A) | Tax geared |
| Failure to produce documents in an enquiry (TMA 1970, s. 97AA): <br>• initial penalty <br>• daily penalty | <br><br>£50 <br>£30/£150[5] |

**Notes**

[1] Interest is charged on penalties not paid when due. The due date is 30 days after the notice of determination of the penalty is issued.

[2] A defence of 'reasonable excuse' may be available.

[3] Late return penalties are cumulative, e.g. for a return six or more months late there are two £100 penalties.

[4] The two fixed £100 penalties are reduced if the total tax payable by assessment is less than the penalty which would otherwise be chargeable.

[5] The lower daily rate applies when determination of the penalty was made by the inspector, the higher when determination was made by the commissioners.

**Partnerships: 2003–04**

| Offence | Penalty[1][2] |
|---|---|
| Late return (TMA 1970, s. 93A)[3][4]:<br>• if return not filed by 1 February 2005<br>• if return not filed by 31 July 2005<br>• for continuing delay on application to the commissioners | <br>£100<br>£100<br><br>Up to £60 per day |
| Failure to notify chargeability | None |
| Incorrect return, accounts and claims made fraudulently or negligently (TMA 1970, s. 95A) | Tax geared |
| Failure to keep and retain tax records (TMA 1970, s. 12B) | Up to £3,000 per year of assessment |
| Failure to produce documents in enquiry (TMA 1970, s. 97AA):<br>• initial penalty<br>• daily penalty | <br><br>£50<br>£30/£150[5] |

**Notes**

[1] Interest is charged on penalties not paid when due. The due date is 30 days after the notice of determination of the penalty is issued.

[2] A defence of 'reasonable excuse' on the part of the representative partner or his successor may be available.

[3] Late return penalties are cumulative, e.g. for a return six or more months late there are two £100 penalties.

[4] Late return penalties apply to each partner (e.g. short delay = £100 per partner).

[5] The lower daily rate applies when determination of the penalty was made by the inspector, the higher when determination was made by the commissioners.

# PAYE thresholds

(*Income Tax (Employments) Regulations* 1993 (SI 1993/744), reg. 28(2))

| Period | Pay days | Amount | |
|---|---|---|---|
| | | Weekly £ | Monthly £ |
| 2003–04 | 6 April 2003 onwards | 89.00 | 385.00 |
| 2002–03 | 6 April 2002 to 5 April 2003 | 89.00 | 385.00 |
| 2001–02 | 6 April 2001 to 5 April 2002 | 87.00 | 378.00 |
| 2000–01 | 6 April 2000 to 5 April 2001 | 84.00 | 365.00 |
| 1999–2000 | 6 April 1999 to 5 April 2000 | 83.00 | 359.60 |
| 1998–99 | 6 April 1998 to 5 April 1999 | 80.50 | 349.50 |
| 1997–98 | 6 April 1997 to 5 April 1998 | 78.00 | 337.00 |

**Note**

Under normal circumstances, employers need not deduct tax for employees who earn less than the above amounts.

# PAYE codes

A  tax code with basic personal allowance plus one half of the Children's Tax Credit. Liability is estimated at the basic rate.

H  tax code with basic personal allowance plus full Children's Tax Credit. Liability estimated at the basic rate.

L  tax code with basic personal allowance.

P  tax code with full personal allowance for those aged 65–74.

J  tax code with full personal allowance for those aged 65–74 plus full married couple's allowance for those aged under 75 and born before 6 April 1935. Liability estimated at basic rate.

Y  tax code with full personal allowance for those aged 75 or over.

T  tax code used where Inland Revenue reviewing other items in tax code. Also used where Inland Revenue asked not to use other codes.

K  total allowances are less than total deductions.

BR, DO, OT, NT mainly used where second source of income and all allowances included in tax code applied to first or main source of income.

# PAYE returns

**Deadlines**

| Forms | Date | Provision | Penalty provisions |
|---|---|---|---|
| P14, P35, P38 and P38A[1] | 19 May following tax year | *Income Tax (Employment) Regulations* 1993 (SI 1993/744), reg. 43 | TMA 1970, s. 98A |
| P60 (to employee) (1996/97 and later years) | 31 May following tax year | *Income Tax (Employments) Regulations* 1993, reg. 39 as amended by *Income Tax (Employments) (Amendment No. 4) Regulations* 1995 | TMA 1970, s. 98A |
| P9D and P11D (1996/97 and later years) | 6 July following tax year | *Income Tax (Employments) Regulations* 1993, reg. 46 as amended by *Income Tax (Employments) (Amendment No. 4) Regulations* 1995 | TMA 1970, s. 98 |
| P46 (Car) (1994/95 and later years) | 3 May, 2 August, 2 November, 2 February | *Income Tax (Employments) Regulations* 1993, reg. 46A | TMA 1970, s. 98 |

**Note**

[1] For 1994–95 onwards, penalties are levied on late returns automatically.

## Penalties that may be imposed for delays

| Forms | Initial | Continuing | Delay exceeds 12 months |
|---|---|---|---|
| P14, P35, P38 and P38A[2] | Up to £1,200[1] per 50 employees | £100 monthly per 50 employees | Penalty not exceeding 100%[1] of the tax or NICs payable for the year of assessment but not paid by 19 April following the end of the year of assessment |
| Forms P9D and P11D | £300 per return[1] | £60 per day[1] | |

**Notes**

[1] This penalty is mitigable.

[2] From 20 May 1995 an automatic non-mitigable penalty applies as follows:

| up to 12 months | £100 per 50 employees chargeable for each month return delayed |
|---|---|
| end 12 months | monthly penalty ceases to accrue additional penalty (not fixed) to be charged |

## Penalties that may be imposed for incorrect returns

| Forms | Provision TMA 1970 | Penalty |
|---|---|---|
| P14, P35, P38 and P38A | s. 98A | Maximum of 100% of tax underpaid (s. 98A(4)) |
| P9D and P11D | s. 98 | Maximum penalty £3,000 (s. 98(2)) |

## Interest on PAYE paid late

Interest on certain late payments of PAYE was introduced from 19 April 1993 in relation to 1992–93 and subsequent tax years (*Income Tax (Employments) Regulations* 1993 (SI 1993/744), reg. 51).

Where an employer has not paid the net tax deductible by him to the collector within 14 days of the end of the tax year, the unpaid tax carries interest at the prescribed rate from the reckonable date until the date of payment. Certain repayments of tax also attract interest.

## Farming and market gardening: relief for fluctuating profits
(ICTA 1988, s. 96)

**Full averaging** (ICTA 1988, s. 96(2))

Applies where profits for either relevant tax year do not exceed 70 per cent of profits for the other year or are nil.

**Marginal averaging** (ICTA 1988, s. 96(3))

Computation of adjustment to the profits of each relevant tax year:
   $3((75\% \text{ H}) - \text{L})$ where:
      H is the higher profit; and
      L is the lower profit.

## Creative artists: relief for fluctuating profits
(ICTA 1988, s. 95A and Sch. 4A)

**Full averaging** (ICTA 1988, Sch. 4A, para. 6(2))

Applies where profits for either relevant tax year do not exceed 70 per cent of profits for the other year or are nil.

**Marginal averaging** (ICTA 1988, Sch. 4A, para. 6(3))

Computation of adjustment to the profits of each relevant tax year where lower profits are between 70 and 75 per cent of higher profits:
   $3((75\% \text{ H}) - \text{L})$
where:
      H is the higher profit; and
      L is the lower profit.

## Personal pension contributions (PPCs) (including stakeholder pensions) and retirement annuity premiums (RAPs)

From 6 April 2001, pension providers can offer stakeholder pensions. The tax regime for personal pensions has been adapted to fit the regime applying to stakeholder pensions.

From 2001–02, contributions can be made to personal schemes *from any source* (not necessarily earnings) up to the level of the 'earnings threshold' for the year. The earnings threshold is a gross figure – the contributor makes a net contribution and the government tops it up by the basic rate of tax, whether or not the payment has been made out of taxed income.

| Tax year | Earnings threshold (gross) – £ | Earnings threshold (net) – £ |
| --- | --- | --- |
| From 2001–02 | 3,600 | 2,808 |

From 2001–02, contributions to personal pensions in excess of the earnings threshold may be made out of *earned income only* to the extent of the age-related percentage of the contributor's net relevant earnings for the year, up to the earnings cap – see tables below.

Tax relief on higher rate contributions is recoverable through self-assessment.

Retirement annuities are unaffected by the 2001 changes in personal pensions.

| Age of taxpayer at the *beginning* of tax year | Limit of allowable payment | |
|---|---|---|
| (ICTA 1988, s. 626, 640(2)) | PPCs % | RAPs % |
| 35 or less | 17.5 | 17.5 |
| 36–45 | 20 | 17.5 |
| 46–50 | 25 | 17.5 |
| 51–55 | 30 | 20 |
| 56–60 | 35 | 22.5 |
| 61–75 | 40 | 27.5 |

*RAPs: Carry-forward* of relief: in calculating the maximum relief deductible in a year, the relief (not premiums/contributions paid) which was not used in an earlier year can be carried forward and used in any of the following six years (ICTA 1988, s. 625, 642). Relief which is carried forward is used on a first-in, first-out basis. This is abolished in respect of PPCs for 2001–02 and subsequent years.

*PPCs: nominating a 'basis year':* Where net relevant earnings exceed the earnings threshold, PPCs in 2001–02 and later years may be based on net relevant earnings in any one of the previous five years (ICTA 1988, s. 646B, 646C). Such 'higher level contributions' may also be made for five years after a year in which earnings have ceased.

*Carry-back* of contributions or premiums: PPCs paid in 2001–02 or any later tax year may be treated as paid in the previous tax year, provided that the contribution is paid on or before 31 January in the later year, and the payer makes an irrevocable election on or before the date of payment. For retirement annuity premiums, and personal pension contributions in 2000–01 and earlier years, an individual can elect to treat all or part of a payment made in one year as if it was paid in the last preceding year, or if he had *no* 'net relevant earnings' in that last preceding year then he can elect to treat it as paid in the last preceding year but one (ICTA 1988, s. 619(4), 641(1); Form 43, PP42 and PP43 in respect of retirement annuity premiums and personal pension contributions respectively).

Where an individual pays both PPCs and RAPs, maximum allowable PPCs (computed by reference to the earnings cap or otherwise) are reduced by qualifying RAPs paid and given relief in the tax year (ICTA 1988, s. 655(1)).

# Personal pension contributions (PPCs) earnings cap

(ICTA 1988, s. 640A, 646A)

| Tax year | Maximum pensionable earnings £ |
|----------|-------------------------------|
| 2003–04 | 99,000 |
| 2002–03 | 97,200 |
| 2001–02 | 95,400 |
| 2000–01 | 91,800 |
| 1999–2000 | 90,600 |
| 1998–99 | 87,600 |
| 1997–98 | 84,000 |

**Note**

The earnings cap also applies for various purposes relating to occupational pension schemes (ICTA 1988, s. 590B, 590C, 592, 594, 599).

# Partners

(ICTA 1988, s. 628)

The earned income limit for a retirement annuity paid to a former partner is 50 per cent of the average of his share of the partnership profits in the best three of the last seven years in which he was a partner.

The former partner's share of the profits in the first six of the last seven years in which he was a partner is increased by the percentage increase in the RPI from the December in the relevant year to the December in the seventh year. The RPI is reproduced on p.72.

## Early retirement ages: retirement annuity contracts and personal pension schemes

The early retirement ages shown in the table below have been agreed by the Revenue under ICTA 1988, s. 620(4)(c) (approval of retirement annuity contracts) and under the provisions of ICTA 1988, s. 634(3)(b) for personal pension schemes. Individuals in other professions or occupations may not normally take benefits from their pension arrangements before age 60 in the case of retirement annuity contracts and before 50 in the case of personal pension schemes, except in the case of retirement owing to illness or disability. For personal pension schemes see also Revenue Booklet IR 76.

| | Retirement age | |
|---|---|---|
| Profession or occupation | Retirement annuity contracts | Personal pension schemes |
| Air pilots | 55 | — |
| Athletes (appearance and prize money) | 35 | 35 |
| Badminton players | 35 | 35 |
| Boxers | 35 | 35 |
| Brass instrumentalists | 55 | — |
| Cricketers | 40 | 40 |
| Croupiers | 50 | — |
| Cyclists | 35 | 35 |
| Dancers | 35 | 35 |
| Divers (saturation, deep sea and free swimming) | 40 | 40 |
| Firemen (part-time) | 55 | — |
| Fishermen (inshore or distant water trawlermen) | 55 | — |
| Footballers | 35 | 35 |
| Golfers (tournament earnings) | 40 | 40 |
| Interdealer brokers | 50 | — |
| Jockeys – flat racing | 45 | 45 |
| – National Hunt | 35 | 35 |
| Martial arts instructors | 50 | — |
| Models | 35 | 35 |
| Moneybroker dealers | 50 | — |
| Moneybroker dealer directors and managers responsible for dealers | 55 | — |
| Motorcycle riders (motocross or road racing) | 40 | 40 |
| Motor racing drivers | 40 | 40 |
| Newscasters (ITV) | 50 | — |
| Nurses, physiotherapists, midwives or health visitors who are females | 55 | — |
| Off-shore riggers | 50 | — |
| Psychiatrists (who are also maximum part-time specialists employed within the National Health Services solely in the treatment of the mentally disordered) | 55 | — |
| Royal Naval reservists | 50 | — |
| Royal Marine reservists non-commissioned | 45 | 45 |
| Rugby League players | 35 | 35 |
| Rugby League referees | 50 | — |

| Profession or occupation | Retirement age | |
|---|---|---|
| | Retirement annuity contracts | Personal pension schemes |
| Skiers (downhill) | — | 30 |
| Singers | 55 | — |
| Speedway riders | 40 | 40 |
| Squash players | 35 | 35 |
| Table tennis players | 35 | 35 |
| Tennis players (including real tennis) | 35 | 35 |
| Territorial Army members | 50 | — |
| Trapeze artistes | 40 | 40 |
| Wrestlers | 35 | 35 |

**Notes**

The pension age shown applies only to pension arrangements funded by contributions paid in respect of the relevant earnings from the occupation or profession carrying that age. If an individual wishes to make pension provisions in respect of another source of relevant earnings to which the pension age shown above does not apply then a separate arrangement, with a pension age within the normal range, must be made. In particular, the ages shown above for professional sportsmen apply only to arrangements made in respect of relevant earnings from activities as professional sportsmen, e.g. tournament earnings, appearance and prize money. They do not apply to relevant earnings from sponsorship or coaching.

# Payments on loss of office and employment

(ICTA 1988, Sch. 11)

| Period | Relief |
|---|---|
| 1997–98 to 2003–04 | £30,000 exempt |

**Notes**

The Revenue will not charge tax on legal costs incurred by a former employee or office holder in a court action to recover compensation for loss of employment, where those costs were recovered under a court order or, under certain circumstances, an out-of-court settlement (ESC A81). The concession does not apply to other professional costs. In relation to ex gratia payments, see SP 13/91, SFO Memoranda No. 104 and 111, ICAEW Technical Release TR 851 and Law Society's *Gazette*, 7 October 1992. (The SFO is now known as the Pensions Schemes Office.)

# Share incentive plans

| | Free Shares | Partnership Shares | Matching Shares[4] | Dividend Shares[5] |
|---|---|---|---|---|
| **Employment before eligibility** | Up to 18 months employment[1] | Up to 6 months (if accumulation period); up to 18 months (if no accumulation period)[1] | Up to 6 months (if accumulation period); up to 18 months (if no accumulation period)[1] | |
| **Limits** | Up to £3,000 per tax year | 2003–04: lower of £1,500 per tax year and 10% of salary for tax year; 2000–01 to 2002–03: lower of £125 per month and 10% of monthly salary | Up to 2 matching shares for each partnership share bought | Dividends reinvested up to £1,500 in a tax year |
| **Minimum amount if stated**[1] | — | At most £10 per month | — | |
| **Performance measures**[1] | Yes | No | No | No |
| **Holding period** | At least 3 years from award[2] | None | At least 3 years from award[2] | 3 years from acquisition |
| **May be forfeited on cessation of employment**[1] | Yes | No | Yes | No |
| **Tax on award** | None | None – tax relief for salary used to buy shares | None | None |
| **Tax on removal of shares from plan within 3 years of award**[3] | On market value when taken out | On market value when taken out | On market value when taken out | Original dividend taxable but in year when shares taken out of plan. |
| **Tax on removal between 3 and 5 years of award**[2] | On lower of: –value at award; & –value on removal | On lower of: –salary used to buy shares; & –value on removal | On lower of: –value at award; & –value on removal | None |
| **Tax on removal after 5 years** | None | None | None | None |
| **CGT on removal – any time** | None | None | None | None |

**Notes**

[1] These conditions can be included at the option of the company.

[2] The holding period may be up to 5 years at the option of the company.

[3] PAYE and NICs will be operated in relation to any income tax charge where the shares are readily convertible assets.

[4] Only awarded to employees who buy partnership shares.

[5] Must be acquired with dividends from plan shares.

# Approved profit sharing schemes

| Maximum value of shares | |
|---|---|
| From 6/4/91 | Greater of £30,000 or 10% of salary, up to £8,000 |

**Notes**

- No further tax-free awards can be made under the APS from April 2002.

With effect from 29 April 1996, the *Finance Act* 1996 reduced the period for which shares must be held in trust from five to three years. For income tax payable on early sale the appropriate percentage is now:

- 100% before the third anniversary;
- 0% on or after third anniversary;
- 50% if the taxpayer ceases to be a director or employee of the grantor (or participating company), or reaches an age between 60 and 75.

The appropriate percentage for excess or unauthorised shares is 100% in every case.

# Company share option plans

The maximum value of shares under option which can be held by an employee at any one time is £30,000.

The price at which the option may be exercised must not be manifestly less than market value at the time the option is granted or an earlier time agreed by the Revenue in writing and provided in the agreement.

# Approved savings-related share option schemes

## Monthly contributions

| Period | Maximum | Minimum |
|---|---|---|
| From 1/4/96 | £250 | £5 to £10[1] |
| From 1/9/91 to 31/3/96 | £250 | £10 |

**Notes**

[1] The company may choose a minimum savings contribution of between £5 and £10. The maximum permissible discount on shares acquired under a scheme is 20% of the market value at the time of the grant of options.

**Bonus and interest payments on termination**

| Date of termination | Amount payable |
|---|---|
| **3-year contract**<br>After at least 1 but less than 3 years | Refund of contributions plus interest at 3% |
| After 3 years | Refund of contributions plus bonus of 3 months' contributions |
| **5-year contract**<br>After at least 1 but less than 5 years | Refund of contributions plus interest at 3% |
| After 5 years | Refund of contributions plus bonus of 9 months' contributions |
| After at least 5 but less than 7 years | Refund of contributions plus bonus of 9 months' contributions and interest at 3% for period after first 5 years |
| After 7 years | Refund of contributions plus bonus of 18 months' contributions |

# Enterprise management incentives (EMI)

| | |
|---|---|
| Qualifying company | From 1 January 2002: gross assets not exceeding £30m<br>Up to 31 December 2001: gross assets not exceeding £15m |
| Maximum options | Up to £100,000 per employee |
| Maximum value of shares subject to EMI options | £3m (before 11 May 2001, £1.5m) |

# Car benefit charges 2002–03 to 2004–05

**Car benefit charges for cars with an approved $CO_2$ emissions figure**

The benefit is calculated on a percentage of the list price of the car appropriate to the level of the car's $CO_2$ emissions, as follows:

- 15% of the list price of cars emitting up to 165 g/km (emissions of carbon dioxide per kilometre) in 2002–03, 155 g/km in 2003–04, 145 g/km in 2004–05;
- increased by 1% per 5 g/km over the 165/155/145 g/km limit;
- capped at 35% of the list price.

If the exact $CO_2$ emissions figure does not end in 0 or 5, it should be rounded *down* to the nearest 5 g/km.

There is a 3% supplement on diesel cars (subject to 35% cap) and discounts for cars using alternative fuels and technologies.

| CO$_2$ emissions in grams per kilometre (g/km) | | | Percentage of car's price to be taxed |
|---|---|---|---|
| 2002–03 | 2003–04 | 2004–05 | |
| 165 | 155 | 145 | 15[1] |
| 170 | 160 | 150 | 16[1] |
| 175 | 165 | 155 | 17[1] |
| 180 | 170 | 160 | 18[1] |
| 185 | 175 | 165 | 19[1] |
| 190 | 180 | 170 | 20[1] |
| 195 | 185 | 175 | 21[1] |
| 200 | 190 | 180 | 22[1] |
| 205 | 195 | 185 | 23[1] |
| 210 | 200 | 190 | 24[1] |
| 215 | 205 | 195 | 25[1] |
| 220 | 210 | 200 | 26[1] |
| 225 | 215 | 205 | 27[1] |
| 230 | 220 | 210 | 28[1] |
| 235 | 225 | 215 | 29[1] |
| 240 | 230 | 220 | 30[1] |
| 245 | 235 | 225 | 31[1] |
| 250 | 240 | 230 | 32[1] |
| 255 | 245 | 235 | 33[2] |
| 260 | 250 | 240 | 34[3] |
| 265 | 255 | 245 | 35[4] |

**Diesel supplements**

[1] Add 3% if car runs solely on diesel.
[2] Add 2% if car runs solely on diesel.
[3] Add 1% if car runs solely on diesel.
[4] Maximum charge, so no diesel supplement.
[5] Budget 2003 announced that the level of CO$_2$ emissions qualifying for the minimum charge in 2005–06 will be reduced to 140 g/km.

**Discounts for cars that run on alternative fuels and technologies**

| Type of car | Discounted charge |
|---|---|
| Battery electric cars | 15% of list price, less 6% discount – i.e. 9% of list price |
| Hybrid electric cars | Appropriate percentage of list price, less 2% discount and a further 1% discount for each full 20 g/km that the $CO_2$ emissions figure is below the qualifying level of the minimum charge for the year (165/155/145 g/km, as in above table). |
| Cars using liquid petroleum gas (LPG) or compressed natural gas (CNG)<br>● Cars running on road fuel gas alone | Appropriate percentage of list price, less 1% discount and a further 1% discount for each full 20 g/km that the $CO_2$ emissions figure is below the qualifying level for the mimimum charge for the year (165/155/145 g/km, as in above table). |
| ● Bi-fuel cars (both gas and petrol) | *Cars first registered on or after 1 January 2000, and approved for running on both petrol and gas*: Appropriate percentage of list price applying to gas $CO_2$ emissions, less 1% discount and a further 1% discount for each full 20 g/km that the $CO_2$ emissions figure is below the qualifying level for the minimum charge for the year (165/155/145 g/km, as in above table).<br>*Cars first registered before 1 January 2000, and petrol cars that are retro-fitted*: Appropriate percentage of list price applying to petrol $CO_2$ emissions, less 1% discount. |

**Car benefit charges for cars with no approved $CO_2$ emissions figure**

The basic car benefit charge will be the car's price multiplied by the percentage charge appropriate to the car's age and engine size (including any diesel supplement).

| Engine size cc | Percentage of car's price to be taxed | |
|---|---|---|
| | **Car first registered before 1 January 1998** | **Car first registered on or after 1 January 1998** |
| 0–1,400 | 15% | 15%[1] |
| 1,401–2,000 | 22% | 25%[1] |
| 2,100+ | 32% | 35%[2] |
| Cars without a cylinder capacity (e.g. rotary engined petrol cars) | 32% | 35% |

**Diesel supplements** (cars registered on or after 1 January 1998 only)
[1] Add 3% if car runs solely on diesel.
[2] Maximum charge, so no diesel supplement.

# Car benefit scales 1999–2000 to 2001–02

| | Percentage of manufacturer's list price (maximum £80,000 price) | |
|---|---|---|
| | Number of cars available concurrently to employee | |
| Age of car at end of tax year under 4 years | First car % | Second and subsequent cars % |
| **Business miles** | | |
| Less than 2,500 miles | 35 | 35 |
| 2,500 miles to 17,999 miles | 25 | 35 |
| 18,000 miles or more | 15 | 25 |
| **Age of car at end of tax year 4 years or more** The percentages above are reduced by ¼. | | |

**Notes**

The cash equivalent benefit and the business mileage limits are reduced proportionately where a car is 'unavailable' for 30 or more consecutive days, or where an employee starts or ceases to have use of the car part way through the year (ICTA 1988, Sch. 6, para. 3, 6 and 9).

The car benefit charge is reduced by any amount which the employee is required to pay as a condition of the car being available for his private use. If the amount exceeds the cash equivalent, the charge is reduced to nil (ICTA 1988, Sch. 6, para. 7).

Generally, the manufacturer's list price is the price of the car published by the manufacturer, distributor or importer of the car when the car was registered, including VAT and any other relevant tax and delivery charge together with the published price for optional accessories (excluding any mobile phone) provided with the car either when first provided or at a later date (subject to a £100 de minimis limit) (ICTA 1988, s. 168A). Where the manufacturer's price list is not available, the Revenue will accept prices taken from published guides (Revenue press release, 27 September 1993). Where an employee contributes towards the capital cost of the car or to qualifying accessories the price is permanently reduced by all capital sums contributed by the employee, subject to an upper limit for the reduction of £5,000 (ICTA 1988, s. 168D(3), (4)). The benefit charge applies to directors and employees earning £8,500 p.a. or over (including benefits) (ICTA 1988, s. 157(1)).

The cost of converting a company car to run on road fuel gases is ignored in calculating the taxable benefit for 1999–2000 and subsequent years of assessment.

# Car benefit scales before 1999–2000

| Age of car at end of tax year under 4 years | Percentage of manufacturer's list price (maximum £80,000 price) | |
|---|---|---|
| | Number of cars available concurrently to employee | |
| | First car % | Second and subsequent cars % |
| **Business miles** | | |
| Less than 2,500 miles | 35 | 35 |
| 2,500 miles to 17,999 miles | 23⅓ | 35 |
| 18,000 miles or more | 11⅔ | 23⅓ |
| **Age of car at end of tax year 4 years or more** The percentages above are reduced by ⅓. | | |

Car benefit scales before 1999–2000 should be read in conjunction with the following notes.

(1) Where business use 2,500 miles or less in relevant year, or additional car(s): increase cash equivalent by 50% (i.e. multiply scale by 1.5) (formerly ICTA 1988, Sch. 6, para. 5).

(2) Where business use 18,000 miles or more in relevant year, reduce cash equivalent by 50% (i.e. divide scale by 2) (formerly ICTA 1988, Sch. 6, para. 3).

(3) The amount of the benefit and the 18,000 and 2,500 mile limits are reduced proportionately if the car was 'unavailable' for 30 or more consecutive days or before or after a particular date (formerly ICTA 1988, Sch. 6, para. 2, 3(2), 5(2) respectively).

(4) The car benefit charge is reduced by any amount which the employee was *required* to pay as a condition of the car being available for his private use. If the amount exceeds the cash equivalent above, the charge is reduced to nil (formerly ICTA 1988, Sch. 6, para. 4).

(5) The car benefit charge applies to directors and employees earning £8,500 p.a. or over (including benefits) (formerly ICTA 1988, s. 157(1)).

**National Insurance contributions on cars:** see p. 45

# Fuel benefit charges from 2003–04

From 6 April 2003, the additional taxable benefit of free fuel provided for a company car is calculated using the same $CO_2$ figures as are used for calculating the company car charge.

For 2003–04, the $CO_2$ percentage figure is applied to a fixed amount of £14,400 (ITEPA 2003, s.150(1)).

The fuel benefit is reduced to nil if the employee is required to make good the full cost of all fuel provided for private use, and does so.

A proportionate reduction is made where the company car is only available for part of the year, where car fuel ceases to be provided part way through the year, and where the benefit of the company car is shared.

# Fuel benefit scales 1997–98 to 2002–03

| Petrol | | Cash equivalent £ |
|---|---|---|
| **2002–03** | **Cylinder capacity** | |
| | 1,400cc or less | 2,240 |
| | 1,401cc–2,000cc | 2,850 |
| | More than 2,000cc | 4,200 |
| | **Original market value; no cylinder capacity** | |
| | Any car | 4,200 |
| **2001–02** | **Cylinder capacity** | |
| | 1,400cc or less | 1,930 |
| | 1,401cc–2,000cc | 2,460 |
| | More than 2,000cc | 3,620 |
| | **Original market value; no cylinder capacity** | |
| | Any car | 3,620 |
| **2000–01** | **Cylinder capacity** | |
| | 1,400cc or less | 1,700 |
| | 1,401cc–2,000cc | 2,170 |
| | More than 2,000cc | 3,200 |
| | **Original market value; no cylinder capacity** | |
| | Any car | 3,200 |
| **1999–2000** | **Cylinder capacity** | |
| | 1,400cc or less | 1,210 |
| | 1,401cc–2,000cc | 1,540 |
| | More than 2,000cc | 2,270 |
| | **Original market value; no cylinder capacity** | |
| | Any car | 2,270 |
| **1998–99** | **Cylinder capacity** | |
| | 1,400cc or less | 1,010 |
| | 1,401cc–2,000cc | 1,280 |
| | More than 2,000cc | 1,890 |
| | **Original market value; no cylinder capacity** | |
| | Any car | 1,890 |
| **1997–98** | **Cylinder capacity** | |
| | 1,400cc or less | 800 |
| | 1,401cc–2,000cc | 1,010 |
| | More than 2,000cc | 1,490 |
| | **Original market value; no cylinder capacity** | |
| | Any car | 1,490 |

| Diesel | Cylinder capacity | Cash equivalent £ |
|--------|-------------------|------------------|
| 2002–03 | 2,000cc or less<br>More than 2,000cc | 2,850<br>4,200 |
| 2001–02 | 2,000cc or less<br>More than 2,000cc | 2,460<br>3,620 |
| 2000–01 | 2,000cc or less<br>More than 2,000cc | 2,170<br>3,200 |
| 1999–2000 | 2,000cc or less<br>More than 2,000cc | 1,540<br>2,270 |
| 1998–99 | 2,000cc or less<br>More than 2,000cc | 1,280<br>1,890 |
| 1997–98 | 2,000cc or less<br>More than 2,000cc | 740<br>940 |

**Notes**

The fuel benefit charge is reduced to nil if the employee is required to make good *all* fuel provided for private use (ICTA 1988, s. 158(6)). The age of the car is irrelevant for the fuel benefit. The benefit does *not* increase if business use was 2,500 miles or less in the year.

## VAT on private fuel:

See p. 137.

## National Insurance contributions on private fuel:

See p. 45.

# Van benefit scales

| | Age of van at end of tax year | |
|---|---|---|
| | Under 4 years £ | 4 years or more £ |
| **1993–94 to 2003–04** | 500 | 350 |

**Notes**

Applies to vehicles weighing 3.5 tonnes or less. The cash equivalent benefit is reduced proportionately where: the van is unavailable for 30 or more consecutive days; where an employee starts or ceases to have use of the van part way through the year; or where the van is a shared van for part of the year. The van benefit charge is reduced by any amount which the employee is required to pay as a condition of the van being available for his private use. If the amount exceeds the cash equivalent, the charge is reduced to nil (ICTA 1988, Sch. 6A). On a claim made by an employee, an alternative calculation may be used. The benefit is calculated as the aggregate of the number of days (including part days) of private use of each van multiplied by £5 (ICTA 1988, Sch. 6A, para. 8(1)–(3)). The van benefit charge applies to directors and employees earning £8,500 p.a. or over (including benefits) (ICTA 1988, s. 159AA). The taxation of vans is under review and is likely to change from 6 April 2004.

# Mobile telephones

From 1991–92 to 1998–99 inclusive, benefit is £200 a year for each mobile telephone available for private use. No benefit arises where the employee is *required* to, and does, make good the full marginal cost of any private use.

From 6 April 1999, this charge has been abolished.

# AA estimated running costs: general

These Schedules are not reproduced for 2003 and subsequent years, as they are not relevant to years for which the fixed profit car scheme has been withdrawn.

# Mileage allowance payments

From 6 April 2002, the new approved mileage rates are statutory maximum amounts that are paid without deducting tax and National Insurance contributions. An employer can decide to pay more or less than the approved mileage rates: any excess is taxable and any shortfall is tax-deductible.

|  | On first 10,000 miles in tax year – rate per mile | On each mile over 10,000 – rate per mile |
|---|---|---|
| Cars and vans | 40p | 25p |
| Motorcycles | 24p | 24p |
| Bicycles | 20p | 20p |

# Revenue authorised mileage rates

The tax-free mileage allowances under the fixed profit car scheme, which applied before 6 April 2002 on a voluntary basis to allowances paid by employers to employees who used their own cars for work, are set out below:

| Tax year | Tax-free rates per mile | | | | |
|---|---|---|---|---|---|
|  | Cars up to 1,000cc | Cars 1,001 to 1,500cc | Cars 1,501 to 2,000cc | Cars over 2,000cc | Composite rate[1] |
| 2001–02 | | | | | |
| Up to 4,000 miles | 40p | 40p | 45p | 63p | 42.5p |
| Over 4,000 miles | 25p | 25p | 25p | 36p | 25p |
| 1997–98 to 2000–2001 | | | | | |
| Up to 4,000 miles | 28p | 35p | 45p | 63p | 40p |
| Over 4,000 miles | 17p | 20p | 25p | 36p | 22.5p |

**Notes**

[1] Irrespective of engine size. Transitional arrangements exist (ICTA 1988, s. 197B) to restrict the extent to which tax liabilities on motor mileage allowances can increase from year to year. Any employee can be taxed individually on the basis of actual motoring expenditure (the statutory basis) if necessary records are kept. If mileage is 8,000, 4,000 miles will be at each rate rather than 8,000 miles at the second rate.

### Authorised rate for pedal cycles

| Tax year | Tax free rate |
|---|---|
| 1999–2000 to 2001–02 | 12p |

### Authorised rate for motor cycles

| Tax year | Tax free rate |
|---|---|
| 2000–01 to 2001–02 | 24p |

# Relocation allowance

### Statutory relief

Tax relief for relocation expenses in relation to payments made or expenses provided in connection with an employee's change of residence where the employee's job or place of work is changed is generally subject to a statutory maximum of £8,000 from 6 April 1993.

# Incidental overnight expenses

Benefits, reimbursements and expenses provided by an employer for employees' minor, personal expenditure whilst on business-related activities requiring overnight accommodation away from home are not taxable provided that the total amount reimbursed, etc. does not exceed the relevant maximum amount(s) per night, multiplied by the number of nights' absence. If the limit is exceeded, the whole amount provided remains taxable.

| From | Authorised maximum per night | |
|---|---|---|
| | In UK £ | Overseas £ |
| 6 April 1995 | 5 | 10 |

# Payroll giving scheme

Employees whose remuneration is subject to deduction of tax at source under PAYE can make donations to charity by requesting that their employers deduct the donations from their pay.

| Year | Maximum donation per year £ |
|---|---|
| 2000–2001 onwards | no maximum |
| 1996–97 to 1999–2000 | 1,200 |
| 1993–94 to 1995–96 | 900 |

Note

The Government provides a 10% supplement on all payroll giving donations for four years from 6 April 2000.

# Individual savings accounts (ISAs)

(ICTA 1988, s. 333)

ISAs started on 6 April 1999 and are guaranteed to run to at least 5 April 2009.

| | Maximum investment per year |
|---|---|
| | **1999–2000 to 2005–06**<br>£ |
| Maxi ISA<br>made up of: | 7,000 |
|   Stocks and shares | up to 7,000 |
|   Cash | up to 3,000 |
|   Life insurance | up to 1,000 |
| Mini ISA types: | |
|   Stocks and shares | 3,000 |
|   Cash | 3,000 |
|   Life insurance | 1,000 |

**Notes**

- A Maxi ISA can include a stocks and shares component, cash component and a life insurance component in a single ISA with one manager. Mini ISAs are separate ISAs, from different managers, for stocks and shares, cash and life insurance.

- Each year an individual can either start new ISAs or can put money into existing ISAs, but only into one Maxi ISA, or one Mini ISA of each type, in any particular tax year.

- To open an ISA an individual has to be aged 18 or over and resident and ordinarily resident in the UK for tax purposes.

- All income and gains derived from investments and life assurance policies within the account are tax free and withdrawals from the account will not attract any tax charge.

- Tax credits attached to dividends from UK companies (which from 6 April 1999 have a value of 10%) are to be paid into the ISA until 5 April 2004. There is a similar entitlement until 5 April 2004 to tax credits attached to dividends which derive from UK equities which back life assurance policies within an ISA. The life assurance company will be able to claim payment of such tax credits.

- On maturity after 5 April 1999, the capital element of a TESSA may be transferred into the cash component of an ISA. Neither the value of any TESSA held, nor the amount of any transfer on maturity, will affect the amount which can be subscribed to an ISA.

- All Personal Equity Plans (PEPs) held at 5 April 1999 can continue to be held as PEPs, but with the same tax advantages as ISAs. Tax-exempt Special Savings Accounts (TESSAs) which were open at 5 April 1999 can continue to be paid into under existing rules for their full five-year life. After that date, capital from maturing TESSAs can be transferred into the cash component of an ISA.

- From 6 April 2001 cash ISAs are extended to sixteen- and seventeen-year-olds. The overall subscription limit of £7,000 is extended until April 2006.


# Settlements on children

(ICTA 1988, s. 660B(5))

Income paid to or for the benefit of a minor child arising from capital provided by a parent is not treated as parents' income if it does not exceed £100 per tax year.

## Enterprise investment scheme (EIS)

(ICTA 1988, s. 289–312)

The EIS applies for 1993–94 and subsequent tax years and is effective in relation to shares issued after 31 December 1993.

| Relief on investment | From | Amount |
|---|---|---|
| Maximum | 1998–99<br>1994–95<br>1993–94 | £150,000<br>£100,000<br>£40,000[1] |
| Minimum investment | 1993–94 | £500 |
| Maximum carry-back to preceding year on investments made between 6 April and 5 October | 1998–99 | The lower of:<br>• 50% of the total relief in respect of the investments; and<br>• £25,000 (£15,000 for 1994–95 to 1997–98) |
| Rate of relief on income tax | 1993–94 | 20% |

**Note**

[1] Applied to an individual's combined investment under the business expansion scheme and the enterprise investment scheme.

The first disposal of shares on which relief has not been withdrawn is exempt from capital gains tax; losses arising from the first disposal of shares are eligible for relief against either income tax or capital gains tax.

Reinvestment relief is available for gains on assets where the disposal proceeds are reinvested in new EIS shares.

Under TCGA 1992, Sch. 5BA, taper relief will be given for the gain on the first investment as though it had been owned throughout the period during which the investor remains invested in EIS companies.

## Venture capital trusts (VCTs)

(ICTA 1988, s. 332A, 842AA, Sch. 15B; TCGA 1992, s. 151A, 151B, Sch. 5C)

A VCT is a type of investment trust, approved by the Revenue on or after 6 April 1995.

**Reliefs:**

• income tax relief of 20% on up to £100,000 per tax year subscribed for new ordinary shares in VCTs is available if the shares are held for five years;
• investors will not be taxed on dividends received from VCTs provided they are within the investment limit exempt from higher rate income tax;
• if an individual disposes of shares in a VCT the gain will be exempt from capital gains tax if the acquisition cost of the shares did not exceed £100,000 in any one year and the shares were held for five years; and
• individuals who subscribe for new ordinary shares in a VCT, on which they have been given income tax relief, will be able to defer CGT on a chargeable gain which arises from the disposal of any assets where the gain is reinvested in the new ordinary shares within the period from one year before, to one year after, the date on which the gain arises.

To obtain the Revenue's approval the trust must satisfy certain conditions. The main ones are as follows:

• it must be a non-close company;
• its shares must be quoted on the stock exchange;
• at least 70% of its income must be wholly or mainly derived from investments in shares or securities; and
• at least 70% (by value) of its total investments must comprise 'qualifying holdings' (broadly, shares in unquoted trading companies).

# Gilt-edged securities held by non-residents (FOTRA securities)

With effect from 6 April 1998, interest on all gilt-edged securities is payable gross (F(No. 2)A 1997, s. 37). Interest on gilts already in issue at that date which is payable under deduction of tax will continue to be payable net unless notice is given to the Bank of England for payment to be made gross. Interest on gilts issued since 5 April 1998 may be paid net, if the holder wishes, again by notice to the Bank of England. Payment gross does not of itself imply that the interest is exempt from tax.

Prior to 6 April 1998, certain specified gilts, and the interest payable on them, were exempt from all UK taxation as long as it was shown that they were in the beneficial ownership of persons who were not ordinarily resident in the UK (so called FOTRA gilts). If interest was payable under deduction of tax, that tax could be reclaimed without recourse to the terms of any applicable double tax treaty. A list of such FOTRA gilts is provided in the table below (excluding securities which have been redeemed).

With effect from 6 April 1998, *all* gilt-edged securities will automatically be given FOTRA status, thereby guaranteeing exemption from tax for holders not ordinarily resident in the UK.

## Description[1]

| Security | Date(s) for repayment |
| --- | --- |
| 9% Conversion Stock 2000 | 3 March 2000 |
| 9% Conversion Stock 2011 | 12 July 2011 |
| 9½% Conversion Stock 2001 | 12 July 2001 |
| 9¾% Conversion Stock 2003 | 7 May 2003 |
| Floating Rate Treasury Stock 1999 | 9 March 1999[1] |
| Floating Rate Treasury Stock 2001 | 8 July 2001 |
| 2½% Index Linked Treasury Stock 2024 | Not later than 17 July 2024 |
| 4⅛% Index Linked Treasury Stock 2030 | 22 July 2030 |
| 4⅜% Index Linked Treasury Stock 2004 | 21 October 2004 |
| 4⅝% Index Linked Treasury Stock 1998 | 27 April 1998 |
| 5½% Treasury Stock 2008/12 | 10 September 2008 to 10 September 2012 |
| 6% Treasury Stock 1999 | 10 August 1999 |
| 6% Treasury Stock 2028 | 7 December 2028 |
| 6¼% Treasury Stock 2010 | 25 November 2010 |
| 6½% Treasury Loan 2003 | 7 December 2003 |
| 6¾% Treasury Loan 2004 | 26 November 2004 |
| 7% Treasury Stock 2001 | 6 November 2001 |
| 7% Treasury Stock 2002 | 7 June 2002 |
| 7¼% Treasury Stock 2007 | 7 December 2007 |
| 7½% Treasury Stock 2006 | 7 December 2006 |
| 7¾% Treasury Stock 2006 | 8 September 2006 |
| 7¾% Treasury Loan 2012/15 | 26 January 2012 to 26 January 2015 |
| 8% Treasury Stock 2000 | 7 December 2000 |
| 8% Treasury Loan 2002/06 | 5 October 2002 to 5 October 2006 |
| 8% Treasury Stock 2003 | 10 June 2003 |
| 8% Treasury Stock 2013 | 27 September 2013 |
| 8% Treasury Stock 2015 | 7 December 2015 |
| 8% Treasury Stock 2021 | 7 June 2021 |
| 8½% Treasury Loan 2000 | 28 January 2000 |
| 8½% Treasury Stock 2005 | 7 December 2005 |
| 8½% Treasury Loan 2007 | 16 July 2007 |
| 8¾% Treasury Loan 2017 | 25 August 2017 |
| 9% Treasury Loan 2008 | 13 October 2008 |
| 9% Treasury Stock 2012 | 6 August 2012 |
| 9½% Treasury Loan 1999 | 15 January 1999 |
| 15½% Treasury Loan 1998 | 30 September 1998 |
| 3½% War Loan | 30 September |

**Note**

[1] List prepared by Inland Revenue Centre for Non-Residents (CNR), St. John's House, Merton Road, Bootle, Merseyside, L69 9BB.

# Official rate of interest

Where an employee or a director earning £8,500 or more a year has outstanding for the whole or part of a year a loan obtained by reason of employment, and no interest or a lesser amount than the official rate is paid for that year, then the cash equivalent is to be treated as an emolument of the employment chargeable to tax.

It was announced in a Revenue press release dated 25 January 2000 that the official rate of interest will be fixed annually in advance. In no circumstances will the rate – once fixed for a year – be increased. It may be reduced if typical interest rates fall during the year.

| Date | Rate | SI Number |
|------|------|-----------|
| From 6 January 2002 to at least 5 April 2004 | 5% | 2001/3860 |
| 6 March 1999 to 5 January 2002 | 6.25% | 1999/419 |
| 6 August 1997 to 5 March 1999 | 7.25% | 1997/1681 |
| 6 November 1996 to 5 August 1997 | 6.75% | 1996/2644 |
| 6 June 1996 to 5 November 1996 | 7% | 1996/1321 |
| 6 February 1996 to 5 June 1996 | 7.25% | 1996/54 |
| 6 October 1995 to 5 February 1996 | 7.75% | 1995/2436 |
| 6 November 1994 to 5 October 1995 | 8% | 1994/2657 |
| 6 January 1994 to 5 November 1994 | 7.5% | 1993/3171 |

**Notes**

There is no tax charge if the employee's cheap or interest-free loans total no more than £5,000.

There is no tax charge in respect of 'non-qualifying loans' totalling no more than £5,000, even where the employee's cheap or interest-free loans total more than £5,000. A 'non-qualifying loan' is one in respect of which interest paid does not qualify for relief under ICTA 1988, s. 353 (ignoring the exclusion of MIRAS loans) and is disallowed in computing the charge under Sch. D, Cases I and II.

## Foreign currency loans

A lower 'official rate' of interest for taxing loans in a foreign currency is set where interest rates in that country are significantly lower than interest rates in the UK. This relief will only apply to a loan in another country's currency, to a person who normally lives in that country and has actually lived there in the year or previous five years. Lower rates of interest for loans in Japanese yen or Swiss francs have been set as follows:

| Loans in Swiss francs | |
|------|------|
| **Date** | **Rate %** |
| From 6 July 1994 | 5.5 |
| From 6 June 1994 to 5 July 1994 | 5.7 |
| **Loans in Japanese yen** | |
| **Date** | **Rate %** |
| From 6 June 1994 | 3.9 |

# Time limits for elections and claims

In the absence of any provision to the contrary, under self-assessment for the purposes of income tax, the normal rule is that claims are to be made within five years from 31 January next following the tax year to which they relate, previously six years from the end of the relevant chargeable period (TMA 1970, s. 43(1)).

For details of time limits relating to payment of income tax, see p. 68.

In certain cases the Board *may* permit an extension of the strict time limit in relation to certain elections and claims.

| Provision | Time limit | Statutory reference |
| --- | --- | --- |
| Actual basis of assessment in second and third years of trade (pre current-year basis) | 7 years from end of the second tax year | Former ICTA 1988, s. 62(2) |
| Actual basis of assessment in fifth and sixth years of a partnership (pre current-year basis) | 7 years from end of the fifth tax year | Former ICTA 1988, s. 62(4) |
| Actual basis of assessment in third year of a Sch. D, Case III–V source (or second year if income first arose on 6 April) (pre current-year basis) | 6 years from end of tax year | Former ICTA 1988, s. 66(1)(c) |
| Averaging of farmers' profits | 12 months from 31 January next following end of the second tax year concerned | ICTA 1988, s. 96(8) |
| Stock transferred to a connected party on cessation of trade to be valued at higher of cost or sale price | 2 years from end of chargeable period in which trade ceased | ICTA 1988, s. 100(1C) |
| Post-cessation expenses relieved against income and chargable gains | 12 months from 31 January next following the tax year | ICTA 1988, s. 109A |
| Elections for transfer of married couple's allowance | Generally before the first tax year for which it is to have effect, and before end of year of marriage | ICTA 1988, s. 257BA(4), (5) |
| Transfer of excess married couple's allowance to wife | 5 years from 31 January next following tax year to which it relates from 1996–97 | ICTA 1988, s. 257BB(5) |
| Election for split of income from investments | Send to Revenue within 60 days of effective date | ICTA 1988, s. 282B(3) |
| Current and preceding year set-off of trading losses | 12 months from 31 January next following tax year loss arose from 1996–97 | ICTA 1988, s. 380; FA 1991, s. 72 |
| Three-year carry-back of trading losses in opening years of trade | 12 months from 31 January next following tax year loss arose from 1996–97 | ICTA 1988, s. 381(1) |
| Carry-forward of trading losses | 5 years from 31 January next following tax year in which loss arose from 1996–97 | ICTA 1988, s. 385(1) |

| Provision | Time limit | Statutory reference |
|---|---|---|
| Carry-back of terminal losses | 5 years from 31 January next following tax year from 1996–97 | ICTA 1988, s. 388(1) |
| Set-off of loss on disposal of shares in unquoted trading company against income | 12 months from 31 January following year in which loss arose from 1996–97 | ICTA 1988, s. 574(1) |
| Carry-back of retirement annuity premiums | 31 January next following tax year in which paid from 1996–97 | ICTA 1988, s. 619(4) |
| Carry-back of personal pension scheme contributions | 31 January next following tax year in which paid from 1996–97 to 2000–2001 | ICTA 1988, s. 641(1), (4) |
| Treat personal pension contribution as paid in preceding tax year | At or before payment made on or before 31 January in tax year | ICTA 1988, s. 641A(1) |
| Certain plant and machinery treated as 'short life' assets | 12 months from 31 January next following the tax year in which ends the chargeable period related to the incurring of the capital expenditure from 1996–97 | CAA 2001, s. 85 |
| Transfer between connected parties of certain assets, eligible for capital allowances, at tax written-down value | 2 years from date of sale | CAA 2001, s. 570(5) |

# National Savings Bank interest

Limit of income tax exemption under ICTA 1988, s. 325 (all years since 1977–78): £70. The exemption is available in respect of separate accounts of husband and wife. The exemption is unavailable in respect of investment deposits.

# Statutory sick pay

Employers are liable to pay SSP in any period of incapacity to work to a maximum of 28 weeks at the SSP rate in force. Statutory sick pay is treated as wages and is subject to PAYE income tax and to National Insurance contributions. Statutory sick pay is not payable for certain periods in which statutory maternity pay is being paid.

The amount of SSP payable to an employee depends on the earnings band into which he or she falls. The earnings bands and the associated SSP payments are as follows:

| Year to | Average gross weekly earnings | Weekly SSP rate[1] £ |
|---|---|---|
| 5 April 2004 | 77.00 or more | 64.35 |
| 5 April 2003 | 75.00 or more | 63.25 |
| 5 April 2002 | 72.00 or more | 62.20 |
| 5 April 2001 | 67.00 or more | 60.20 |
| 5 April 2000 | 66.00 or more | 59.55 |
| 5 April 1999 | 64.00 or more | 57.70 |

**Note**

[1] The daily rate of SSP is ascertained by dividing the weekly rate by the number of qualifying days in the week (beginning on Sunday), then multiplying by the number of qualifying days of incapacity in the week, rounded up to the nearest penny.

### Maximum entitlement

An employee reaches his maximum entitlement to SSP in one spell of incapacity when he has been paid 28 times the appropriate rate, i.e. £64.35 × 28 = £1,801.80.

# Statutory maternity pay

From 6 April 2003 new maternity pay rules are to apply. The most important changes are that the pay period is to be extended from 18 weeks to a maximum of 26 weeks and the period of notice which must be given to the employer for the maternity pay period start date increases from 21 days to 28 days. During the first 6 weeks when statutory maternity pay is payable the earnings related rate will no longer be subject to the flat rate.

| Year | First 6 weeks | Remaining weeks |
|---|---|---|
| From 6 April 2003[1] | 90% average weekly earnings | Lower of £100.00 or earnings related rate |

**Note**

[1] Where the maternity pay period spans 6 April 2003 there is a minimum of £75.00 a week.

**2002–03 and earlier years are set out below:**

Statutory maternity pay (SMP) is paid for a maximum of 18 weeks to employees with average weekly earnings of at least £75 a week (in 2002–03).

| Higher weekly rate:[1] | ⁹/₁₀ of employee's average weekly earnings | |
|---|---|---|
| Lower weekly rate:[2] | from 6 April 2002 | £75.00 |
| | from 6 April 2001 | £62.60 |
| | from 6 April 2000 | £62.20 |
| | from 6 April 1999 | £59.55 |
| | from 6 April 1998 | £57.70 |
| | from 6 April 1997 | £55.70 |

**Notes**

[1] Payable for the first six weeks of payment.

[2] Payable for the remaining weeks of the Maternity Pay Period.

# Taxable state benefits

The following benefits are liable to income tax (ICTA 1988, s. 617):

| Benefit | Weekly rate from | |
|---|---|---|
| | 7 April 2003 £ | 8 April 2002 £ |
| **Industrial death benefit:** | | |
| **Widow's pension** | | |
| Permanent rate — higher | 77.45 | 75.50 |
| lower | 23.24 | 22.65 |
| **Invalid care allowance** | | |
| Standard rate | 43.15 | 42.45 |
| **Incapacity benefit (long term)** | | |
| Rate | 72.15 | 70.95 |
| Increase for age: | | |
| higher rate | 15.15 | 14.90 |
| lower rate | 7.60 | 7.45 |
| **Incapacity benefit (short term)** | | |
| Higher rate: | | |
| under pensionable age[1] | 64.35 | 63.25 |
| over pensionable age[1] | 72.15 | 70.95 |
| **Non-contributory retirement pension** | | |
| Standard rate | 46.35 | 45.20 |
| Age addition (at age 80) | 0.25 | 0.25 |
| **Retirement pension** | | |
| Standard rate | 77.45 | 75.50 |
| Age addition (at age 80) | 0.25 | 0.25 |
| **Jobseeker's allowance** | | |
| See p. 41 | | |
| **SSP and SMP** | | |
| See p. 37 | | |
| **Widow's pension**[2] | | |
| Pension (standard rate) | 77.45 | 75.50 |
| **Widowed parent allowance and bereavement allowance** | 77.45 | 75.50 |
| **Dependent adults** | | |
| with retirement pension | 46.35 | 45.20 |
| with invalid care allowance | 25.80 | 25.35 |

**Notes**

[1] Pensionable age is 60 for women, 65 for men. From 6 April 2020 the state pension age for women will be 65, the same as for men. From 2010 women's state pension age will be gradually increased to bring it up to age 65 by 2020.

[2] Bereavement allowance replaced widow's pension from 9 April 2001 for all new claims by widows and widowers.

# State benefits: not taxable

The following benefits are not liable to income tax:

- Attendance allowance
- Back to work bonus
- Child benefit
- Child maintenance bonus
- Christmas bonus
- Constant attendance allowance
- Council tax benefit
- Council tax benefit extended payment
- Criminal injuries compensation
- Disability living allowance
- Education welfare benefits
- Employment rehabilitation allowance
- Guardian's allowance
- Housing benefit
- Housing benefit extended payment
- Incapacity benefit (short-term, lower rate)
- Income support
- Industrial injuries disablement benefit
- Jobseeker's allowance, amounts above personal or couple rate
- Lone parent's benefit run-on
- Maternity allowance
- Medical expenses incurred in the European Economic Area
- Motability
- Pneumoconiosis, byssinosis and misc. disease scheme benefits
- Reduced earnings allowance
- Statutory redundancy payments
- Retirement allowance (payable under industrial injuries scheme)
- Severe disablement allowance (withdrawn for new claimants from 6 April 2001)
- Social fund payments — budgeting loan, cold weather payment, community care grant, crisis loan, funeral payment, maternity payment, winter fuel payments
- Vaccine damage
- War disablement pension
- War pensioner's mobility supplement
- War widow's pension
- Widow's payment
- Widowed mother's allowance child dependency increase
- Worker's compensation (supplementation) scheme

| Benefit | Weekly rate (£) | |
|---|---|---|
| | from 7 April 2003 | from 8 April 2002 |
| **Attendance allowance** | | |
| Higher rate (day and night) | 57.20 | 56.25 |
| Lower rate (day or night) | 38.20 | 37.65 |
| **Child benefit** | | |
| For the eldest qualifying child | 16.05 | 15.75 |
| Lone parent[4] | 17.55 | 17.55 |
| For each other child | 10.75 | 10.55 |
| **Christmas bonus** | | |
| Single annual payment | 10.00 | 10.00 |
| **Constant attendance allowance** | | |
| Exceptional rate | 93.60 | 92.00 |
| Intermediate rate | 70.20 | 69.00 |
| Normal maximum rate | 46.80 | 46.00 |
| Exceptionally severe disablement allowance | 46.80 | 46.00 |
| **Maternity allowance** | | |
| Standard rate | 100.00 | 75.00 |
| **Guardian's allowance**[1] | | |
| Eldest qualifying child | 9.55 | 9.65 |
| Each other child | 11.55 | 11.35 |
| **Disability living allowance (care component)** | | |
| Higher rate | 57.20 | 56.25 |
| Middle rate | 38.30 | 37.65 |
| Lower rate | 15.15 | 14.90 |
| **Disability living allowance (mobility component)** | | |
| Higher rate | 39.95 | 39.30 |
| Lower rate | 15.15 | 14.90 |
| **Income support (see below)** | | |
| **Incapacity benefit (short term)**[4] | | |
| Lower rate: | | |
| under pensionable age[3] | 54.40 | 53.50 |
| over pensionable age[3] | 69.20 | 68.05 |

**Notes**

[1] Also child special allowance, and child dependency increases with retirement pension, widow's benefit, short-term incapacity benefit at the higher rate and long-term incapacity benefit, invalid care allowance, severe disablement allowance, higher rate individual death benefit, unemployability supplement and short-term incapacity benefit if beneficiary over pension age.

[2] Incapacity benefit replaced invalidity benefit and sickness benefit from 6 April 1995. It is taxable, under Sch. E, except for short-term benefit payable at the lower rate. It is not taxable, however, if recipient started receiving invalidition benefit or sickness benefit before 6 April 1995 and has continued receiving incapacity benefit since then.

[3] Pensionable age is 60 for women, 65 for men. From 6 April 2020 the state pension age for women will be 65, the same as for men. From 2010 women's state pension age will be gradually increased to bring it up to age 65 by 2020.

[4] Withdrawn from 6 July 1998 except for those who have been receiving child benefit (lone parent) since before that date and whose circumstances have not changed; or those who, since before that date, have been receiving income support or income-based jobseeker's allowance which included the lone parent rate of family premium, or a disability premium, or a pension premium, and who have just come off benefit to start work.

# Income support and jobseeker's allowance

Income support is not taxable.

The personal or couple rate of jobseeker's allowance is taxable. Any amounts of jobseeker's allowance payable above the personal or couple rate (e.g. premiums) are not taxable.

## Rate of income support

| | Weekly rate £ | |
|---|---|---|
| | From 7 April 2003 | From 8 April 2002 |
| **Single** | | |
| Aged 16 to 17 | 32.90 | 32.50 |
| Aged 16 to 17 (higher rate) | 43.25 | 42.70 |
| Aged 18 to 24 | 43.25 | 42.70 |
| Aged 25 and over | 54.65 | 53.95 |
| **Couple** | | |
| Both aged 16 to 17 | 65.30 | 64.45 |
| One aged 18 and over | 85.75 | 84.65 |
| **Lone parent** | | |
| Aged 16 to 17 | 32.90 | 32.50 |
| Aged 16 to 17 (higher rate) | 43.25 | 42.70 |
| Aged 18 and over | 54.65 | 53.95 |
| **Dependent children** | | |
| From birth to age 16[1] | 38.50 | 33.50[3] |
| Age 16 to 19[2] | 38.50 | 34.30[3] |

**Notes**

[1] From birth to September following 16th birthday.

[2] From September following 16th birthday to the day before 19th birthday.

[3] Rates increased in October 2002 to £37.00 and £37.80 respectively.

## Rates of jobseeker's allowance

| | Weekly rate £ | |
|---|---|---|
| | From 7 April 2003 | From 8 April 2002 |
| **Contribution based JSA, personal allowance** | | |
| Aged under 18 | 32.90 | 32.50 |
| Aged 18 to 24 | 43.25 | 42.70 |
| Aged 25 and over | 54.65 | 53.95 |
| **Income based JSA, personal allowance**[3] | | |
| Aged under 18 | 32.90 | 32.50 |
| Aged 18 to 24 | 43.25 | 42.70 |
| Aged 25 and over | 54.65 | 53.95 |
| **Couple** | | |
| Both under 18 | 32.90 | 32.50 |
| Both under 18, one disabled | 43.25 | 42.70 |
| Both under 18, with responsibility for a child | 65.30 | 64.45 |
| One under 18, one 18 to 24 | 43.25 | 42.70 |
| One under 18, one 25 or over | 54.65 | 53.95 |
| Both 18 or over | 85.75 | 84.65 |
| **Dependent children**[4] | | |
| From birth to age 16 | 38.50 | 33.50 |
| Age 16 to 19 | 38.50 | 34.30 |

**Notes**

[3] Also lone parent rate.

[4] See footnotes 1, 2 and 3 under Rate of income support above.

**Income support and jobseeker's allowance – premiums**

| Premium | Weekly rate £ | |
| --- | --- | --- |
| | From 7 April 2003 | From 8 April 2002 |
| Family | 15.75 | 14.75 |
| Family (lone parent rate) | 15.90 | 15.90 |
| Pensioner (single) | 47.45 | 44.20 |
| Pensioner (couple) | 70.05 | 65.15 |
| Pensioner (enhanced) – single | 47.45 | 44.20 |
| Pensioner (enhanced) – couple | 70.05 | 65.15 |
| Pensioner (higher) – single | 47.45 | 44.20 |
| Pensioner (higher) – couple | 70.05 | 65.15 |
| Disability – single | 23.30 | 23.00 |
| Disability – couple | 33.25 | 32.80 |
| Severe disability – single | 42.95 | 42.25 |
| Severe disability –couple (one qualifies) | 42.95 | 42.25 |
| Severe disability – couple (both qualify) | 85.90 | 84.50 |
| Enhanced disability – single | 11.40 | 11.25 |
| Enhanced disability – couple | 16.45 | 16.25 |
| Disabled child | 41.30 | 35.50 |
| Enhanced disability – child | 16.60 | 11.25 |
| Carer | 25.10 | 24.80 |

# NATIONAL INSURANCE CONTRIBUTIONS

## NIC rates: general

There are five classes of National Insurance contributions payable according to the individual circumstances of the payer.

## Class 1 contributions

Class 1 contributions are earnings related. An employee and his employer must pay such contributions if his earnings reach the lower limit. Employees' contributions are paid on all earnings up to an upper limit.

The reduced rate applies to married women or widows with a valid certificate of election. Men over 65 and women over 60 pay no primary contributions, though employers still pay the secondary contribution, usually at the non-contracted out rate, regardless of the previous category of contribution liability. Children under 16 and their employers pay no contributions.

## Class 1 contributions

| Class 1 primary (employee) contributions 2004–05[1] | |
|---|---|
| Lower earnings limit (LEL)[2] | £79 weekly<br>£343 monthly<br>£4,108 yearly |
| Primary threshold | £91 weekly<br>£395 monthly<br>£4,732 yearly |
| Rate on earnings up to primary threshold | 0% |
| *Not contracted-out* rate on earnings between primary threshold and upper earnings limit (UEL) | 11% |
| *Contracted-out* rate on earnings between primary threshold and UEL | 9.4% |
| *Reduced rate* on earnings between primary threshold and UEL[3] | 4.85% (£91.01–£610 weekly);<br>1% above £610 |
| Upper earnings limit (UEL) | £610 weekly<br>£2,644 monthly<br>£31,720 yearly |

| Class 1 primary (employee) contributions 2003–04[1] | |
|---|---|
| Lower earnings limit (LEL)[2] | £77 weekly<br>£334 monthly<br>£4,004 yearly |
| Primary threshold | £89 weekly<br>£385 monthly<br>£4,628 yearly |
| Rate on earnings up to primary threshold | 0% |
| *Not contracted-out* rate on earnings between primary threshold and upper earnings limit (UEL) | 11% |
| *Contracted-out* rate on earnings between primary threshold and UEL | 9.4% |
| *Reduced rate* on earnings between primary threshold and UEL[3] | 4.85% (£89.01–£595 weekly);<br>1% above £595 |
| Upper earnings limit (UEL) | £595 weekly<br>£2,578 monthly<br>£30,940 yearly |

| Class 1 primary (employee) contributions 2002–03[1] | |
|---|---|
| Lower earnings limit (LEL)[2] | £75 weekly<br>£325 monthly<br>£3,900 yearly |
| Primary threshold | £89 weekly<br>£385 monthly<br>£4,615 yearly |
| Rate on earnings up to primary threshold | 0% |
| *Not contracted-out* rate on earnings between primary threshold and upper earnings limit (UEL) | 10% |
| *Contracted-out* rate on earnings between primary threshold and UEL | 8.4% |
| *Reduced rate* on earnings between primary threshold and UEL[3] | 3.85% |
| Upper earnings limit (UEL) | £585 weekly<br>£2,535 monthly<br>£30,420 yearly |

| Class 1 primary (employee) contributions 2001–02[1] | |
|---|---|
| Lower earnings limit (LEL)[2] | £72 weekly<br>£312 monthly<br>£3,744 yearly |
| Primary threshold | £87 weekly<br>£378 monthly<br>£4,535 yearly |
| Rate on earnings up to primary threshold | 0% |
| *Not contracted-out* rate on earnings between primary threshold and upper earnings limit (UEL) | 10% |
| *Contracted-out* rate on earnings between primary threshold and UEL | 8.4% |
| *Reduced rate* on earnings between primary threshold and UEL[3] | 3.85% |
| Upper earnings limit | £575 weekly<br>£2,491 monthly<br>£29,900 yearly |

**Notes**

[1] Class 1 contributions are earnings related. Employees must pay primary Class 1 contributions on that part of their earnings which exceeds the primary threshold, up to the upper earnings limit.

[2] For 1999–2000 and later years, earnings from the LEL, up to and including the primary threshold, will count towards the employee's basic 'flat rate' state pension, even though no contributions will have been paid on those earnings. Similarly, earnings between the LEL and the primary threshold will count towards the employee's entitlement to certain benefits including the additional pension (SERPS) or, from April 2002, the second state pension.

[3] The reduced rate applies to married women or widows with a valid certificate of election. Men over 65 and women over 60 pay no primary contributions, though employers still pay the secondary contribution at the usual rate. People under 16 and their employers pay no contributions.

| Class 1 secondary (employer) contributions 2004–05[1] | |
|---|---|
| Earnings threshold | £91 weekly<br>£395 monthly<br>£4,732 yearly |
| *Not contracted-out* rate | 12.8% above earnings threshold |
| *Contracted-out* rate[2] | 9.3% for salary-related (COSR) and 11.8% for money-purchase (COMP) schemes (including 3.5% and 1.0% rebates for earnings from LEL to secondary threshold), then 12.8% above UEL |

| Class 1 secondary (employer) contributions 2003–04[1] | |
|---|---|
| Earnings threshold | £89 weekly<br>£385 monthly<br>£4,615 yearly |
| *Not contracted-out* rate | 12.8% above earnings threshold |
| *Contracted-out* rate[2] | 9.3% for salary-related (COSR) and 11.8% for money-purchase (COMP) schemes (including 3.5% and 1.0% rebates for earnings from LEL to secondary threshold), then 12.8% above UEL |

| Class 1 secondary (employer) contributions 2002–03[1] | |
|---|---|
| Earnings threshold | £89 weekly<br>£385 monthly<br>£4,615 yearly |
| *Not contracted-out* rate | 11.8% above earnings threshold |
| *Contracted-out* rate[2] | 8.3% for salary-related (COSR) and 10.8% for money-purchase (COMP) schemes (including 3.5% and 1.0% rebates for earnings from LEL to secondary threshold), then 11.8% above UEL |

| Class 1 secondary (employer) contributions 2001–02[1] | |
|---|---|
| Earnings threshold | £87 weekly<br>£378 monthly<br>£4,535 yearly |
| *Not contracted-out* rate | 11.9% above earnings threshold |
| *Contracted-out* rates[2] | 8.9% for salary-related (COSR) and 11.3% for money-purchase (COMP) schemes (including 3% and 0.6% rebates for earnings from LEL to earnings threshold), then 11.9% above UEL |

**Notes**

[1] Class 1 contributions are earnings related. Employers must pay secondary Class 1 contributions on that part of an employee's earnings which exceeds the earnings threshold, without limit (i.e. without capping).

[2] With contracted-out salary related (COSR) schemes there is an employer's NIC rebate of a percentage of earnings above the employer's earnings threshold, up to and including the upper earnings limit. With contracted-out money purchase (COMP) schemes there is an employer's NIC rebate of a percentage of earnings above the employer's earnings threshold, up to and including the upper earnings limit, and a further age-related rebate is paid by the Inland Revenue National Insurance Contributions Office directly to the scheme.

**Class 1 contracted-out rebates 2002–03 and 2003–04**

|  | COSR<br>(salary related)<br>% | COMP<br>(money purchase)<br>% |
|---|---|---|
| Employees | 1.6 | 1.6 |
| Employers | 3.5 | 1.0 + age-related<br>percentage |

**Class 1 contracted-out rebates 2001–02**

|  | COSR<br>(salary related)<br>% | COMP<br>(money purchase)<br>% |
|---|---|---|
| Employees | 1.6 | 1.6 |
| Employers | 3 | 0.6 + age-related<br>percentage |

**Appropriate age-related percentages of earnings exceeding the lower earnings limit but not the upper earnings limit**

| Age on last day of preceding tax year | Appropriate age-related percentages for the tax year | | | | |
|---|---|---|---|---|---|
|  | 2002–03 | 2003–04 | 2004–05 | 2005–06 | 2006–07 |
| 15 | 2.6 | 2.6 | 2.6 | 2.6 | 2.6 |
| 16 | 2.6 | 2.6 | 2.6 | 2.6 | 2.6 |
| 17 | 2.7 | 2.7 | 2.7 | 2.7 | 2.7 |
| 18 | 2.7 | 2.7 | 2.7 | 2.7 | 2.7 |
| 19 | 2.8 | 2.8 | 2.8 | 2.8 | 2.8 |
| 20 | 2.8 | 2.8 | 2.8 | 2.8 | 2.8 |
| 21 | 2.9 | 2.9 | 2.9 | 2.9 | 2.9 |
| 22 | 2.9 | 2.9 | 2.9 | 2.9 | 3.0 |
| 23 | 3.0 | 3.0 | 3.0 | 3.0 | 3.0 |
| 24 | 3.1 | 3.1 | 3.1 | 3.1 | 3.1 |
| 25 | 3.1 | 3.1 | 3.1 | 3.1 | 3.1 |
| 26 | 3.2 | 3.2 | 3.2 | 3.2 | 3.2 |
| 27 | 3.2 | 3.2 | 3.2 | 3.2 | 3.2 |
| 28 | 3.3 | 3.3 | 3.3 | 3.3 | 3.3 |
| 29 | 3.4 | 3.4 | 3.4 | 3.4 | 3.4 |
| 30 | 3.4 | 3.4 | 3.4 | 3.4 | 3.4 |
| 31 | 3.6 | 3.6 | 3.6 | 3.6 | 3.6 |

| Age on last day of preceding tax year | Appropriate age-related percentages for the tax year | | | | |
|---|---|---|---|---|---|
| | 2002–03 | 2003–04 | 2004–05 | 2005–06 | 2006–07 |
| 32 | 3.6 | 3.6 | 3.6 | 3.6 | 3.6 |
| 33 | 3.7 | 3.7 | 3.7 | 3.7 | 3.7 |
| 34 | 3.8 | 3.8 | 3.8 | 3.8 | 3.8 |
| 35 | 3.8 | 3.8 | 3.8 | 3.8 | 3.8 |
| 36 | 3.9 | 3.9 | 3.9 | 3.9 | 3.9 |
| 37 | 4.0 | 4.0 | 4.0 | 4.0 | 4.0 |
| 38 | 4.1 | 4.1 | 4.1 | 4.1 | 4.1 |
| 39 | 4.1 | 4.1 | 4.1 | 4.1 | 4.1 |
| 40 | 4.3 | 4.2 | 4.2 | 4.2 | 4.2 |
| 41 | 4.4 | 4.4 | 4.3 | 4.3 | 4.3 |
| 42 | 4.6 | 4.5 | 4.4 | 4.4 | 4.4 |
| 43 | 4.8 | 4.7 | 4.6 | 4.5 | 4.4 |
| 44 | 5.0 | 4.9 | 4.8 | 4.7 | 4.6 |
| 45 | 5.3 | 5.1 | 5.0 | 4.9 | 4.8 |
| 46 | 5.5 | 5.4 | 5.3 | 5.1 | 5.0 |
| 47 | 6.0 | 5.6 | 5.5 | 5.4 | 5.3 |
| 48 | 6.8 | 6.1 | 5.7 | 5.6 | 5.5 |
| 49 | 7.8 | 6.9 | 6.2 | 5.8 | 5.7 |
| 50 | 9.0 | 7.9 | 7.1 | 6.4 | 5.9 |
| 51 | 10.3 | 9.1 | 8.1 | 7.2 | 6.5 |
| 52 | 10.5 | 10.5 | 9.3 | 8.2 | 7.4 |
| 53 | 10.5 | 10.5 | 10.5 | 9.5 | 8.4 |
| 54 | 10.5 | 10.5 | 10.5 | 10.5 | 9.7 |
| 55 | 10.5 | 10.5 | 10.5 | 10.5 | 10.5 |
| 56 | 10.5 | 10.5 | 10.5 | 10.5 | 10.5 |
| 57 | 10.5 | 10.5 | 10.5 | 10.5 | 10.5 |
| 58 | 10.5 | 10.5 | 10.5 | 10.5 | 10.5 |
| 59 | 10.5 | 10.5 | 10.1 | 9.7 | 9.3 |
| 60 | 10.5 | 10.5 | 10.5 | 10.3 | 9.9 |
| 61 | 10.5 | 10.5 | 10.5 | 10.5 | 10.5 |
| 62 | 10.5 | 10.5 | 10.5 | 10.5 | 10.5 |
| 63 | 10.5 | 10.5 | 10.5 | 10.5 | 10.5 |

## Class 1A contributions

From 6 April 2000, employers (but not employees) pay NICs on an annual basis on taxable benefits in kind provided to employees earning at the rate of £8,500 pa or more or to directors. The Class 1A rate for 2003–04 is 12.8 per cent. Contributions for the year are due by 19 July following the end of the tax year to which they relate.

Prior to 6 April 2000, employers (but not employees) paid NICs on an annual basis on cars or fuel provided for the private use of employees earning at the rate of £8,500 pa or more or for directors. The liability is calculated on the income tax car and fuel scale rates (see p. 18 and p. 22 respectively).

## Return deadlines for Class 1 and 1A contributions

| Forms | Date | Penalty provision |
|---|---|---|
| End of year returns P14, P35, P38 and P38A | 19 May following year of assessment | TMA 1970, s. 98A |
| P11D(b) | 6 July following year of assessment | SI 2001/1004, reg. 81(2) |

**Notes**

In cases of PAYE and NIC default there are provisions to prevent double charging. Class 1A contributions are recorded annually in arrears. Penalties will only be imposed if there is a delay in the submission of the relevant year's PAYE return.

## Class 1B contributions

From 6 April 1999 Class 1B contributions are payable by employers on the amount of emoluments in a PAYE settlement agreement which are chargeable to Class 1 or Class 1A NICs, together with the total amount of income tax payable under the agreement. Class 1B contributions are charged at a rate equal to the secondary rate of NICs (12.8 per cent in 2003–04), with power for the Secretary of State to alter the rate by statutory instrument; but not so as to increase it to more than two per cent above the rate applicable at the end of the preceding year.

## Class 2 contributions

Class 2 contributions are paid at a flat rate by a self-employed person unless he has applied for and been granted exception because his earnings are below the exception (SEE) limit for Class 2 contributions. If a person is excepted, he may still pay the contributions voluntarily to keep up his right to the benefits they provide.

A person who becomes, or ceases to be, liable or entitled to pay Class 2 contributions must notify the Revenue. A penalty of £100 is exigible if they fail to notify the Revenue by the end of the third calendar month following the date on which they start up in business, unless they have a reasonable excuse for not notifying, or during the whole of that period their earnings do not exceed the small earnings exception for Class 2.

| Tax year | Weekly contribution | | | Small earnings exception limit £ |
| | Normal rate £ | Share fishermen £ | Volunteer development workers £ | |
|---|---|---|---|---|
| 2004–05 | 2.05 | 2.70 | 3.95 | 4,215 |
| 2003–04 | 2.00 | 2.65 | 3.85 | 4,095 |
| 2002–03 | 2.00 | 2.65 | 3.75 | 4,025 |
| 2001–02 | 2.00 | 2.65 | 3.60 | 3,955 |

## Class 3 contributions

Class 3 contributions are paid voluntarily by persons not liable for contributions, or who have been excepted from Class 2 contributions, or whose contribution record is insufficient to qualify for benefits. They are paid at a flat rate.

| Tax year | Weekly contribution rate £ | Earnings factor for each contribution in col. 2 £ |
|---|---|---|
| 2004–05 | 7.15 | 79.00 |
| 2003–04 | 6.95 | 77.00 |
| 2002–03 | 6.85 | 75.00 |
| 2001–02 | 6.75 | 72.00 |

## Class 4 contributions

Self-employed people whose profits or gains are over a certain amount have to pay Class 4 contributions as well as Class 2 contributions. These contributions are earnings related and paid on earnings between the lower and upper earnings limits.

| Tax year | Percentage rate £ | Annual lower earnings limit £ | Annual upper earnings limit £ | Maximum contribution £ |
|---|---|---|---|---|
| 2004–05 | 8% (£4,745–£31,720) 1% above £31,720 | 4,745 | 31,720 | — |
| 2003–04 | 8% (£4,615–£30,940) 1% above £30,940 | 4,615 | 30,940 | — |
| 2002–03 | 7.0 | 4,615 | 30,420 | 1,806.35 |
| 2001–02 | 7.0 | 4,535 | 29,900 | 1,775.55 |

One-half of Class 4 contributions may be deducted in computing total income for income tax purposes (ICTA 1988, s. 617(5)).

## Annual maximum contributions for years up to 2002–03

### Note

Following the introduction of additional primary Class 1 contributions on earnings above the upper earnings limit from 6 April 2003, the annual maximum applicable to each individual will vary according to their earnings. It is therefore no longer possible to calculate a single figure which will be of universal application.

For the limit placed on a person's total NIC liability under Class 1, Class 2 and Class 4, see the centre column of the table below.

Where a person's total Class 1 and Class 2 contributions in a tax year are less than the figure given in the second column in the table, his Class 4 liability is limited to the difference between that total and the figure in the third column.

| Tax year | Overall maximum £ | Class 4 maximum £ |
|---|---|---|
| 2002–03 | 2,628.80 | 1,912.35 |
| 2001–02 | 2,586.40 | 1,881.55 |

## Interest on overdue Class 1, 1A, 1B and 4 National Insurance contributions: 2004–05

(SSCBA 1992, Sch. 1, para. 6; s. 15(2))

| Contributions | Due date | Reckonable date for interest |
|---|---|---|
| Class 1 | 19 April 2005 | 19 April 2005 |
| Class 1A direct payment method | 19 July 2005 | 19 April 2006 |
| Class 1A alternative method | 19 July 2005 | 19 July 2005 |
| Class 1B | 19 October 2005 | 19 October 2005 |
| Class 4 | As for self-assessment (see p. 66) | |

Interest is paid on repayments of overpaid Class 1, 1A, 1B and 4 contributions from the dates shown above until repayment (see p. 69).

# TAXATION OF COMPANIES

## Corporation tax rates

The rates of corporation tax for recent financial years are given below:

| Financial year | Full rate % | Small companies' rate % | Profit limit for small companies' rate (lower limit) | Profit limit for small companies' marginal relief (upper limit) | Marginal relief fraction for small companies | Starting rate % | Profit limit for starting rate (lower limit) | Profit limit for starting rate marginal relief (upper limit) | Marginal relief fraction for starting rate |
|---|---|---|---|---|---|---|---|---|---|
| 2003 | 30 | 19 | 300,000 | 1,500,000 | 11/400 | — | 10,000 | 50,000 | 19/400 |
| 2002 | 30 | 19 | 300,000 | 1,500,000 | 11/400 | — | 10,000 | 50,000 | 19/400 |
| 2001 | 30 | 20 | 300,000 | 1,500,000 | 1/40 | 10 | 10,000 | 50,000 | 1/40 |
| 2000 | 30 | 20 | 300,000 | 1,500,000 | 1/40 | 10 | 10,000 | 50,000 | 1/40 |
| 1999 | 30 | 20 | 300,000 | 1,500,000 | 1/40 | — | — | — | — |
| 1998 | 31 | 21 | 300,000 | 1,500,000 | 1/40 | — | — | — | — |
| 1997 | 31 | 21 | 300,000 | 1,500,000 | 1/40 | — | — | — | — |

**Notes**

[1] The lower and upper limits for the small companies' rate and the small companies' marginal relief, as well as the similar lower and upper limits for the starting rate, are reduced proportionally:

- for accounting periods of less than 12 months; and
- in the case of associated companies, by dividing the limits by the total number of non-dormant associated companies.

[2] The full rate of corporation tax for the financial year 2004 has been set at 30%.

[3] 'Close investment holding companies' do not receive the benefit of the small companies' rate or the starting rate and so are taxable entirely at the full rate regardless of the level of their profits.

## Effective marginal rates

For marginal small companies' relief and marginal starting rate relief, there is an effective rate of tax in the margin, i.e. between the lower and upper limits given for each in the preceding table, which *exceeds* the full rate. These marginal rates are not prescribed by statute, but are derived from the appropriate corporation tax rates and fractions. The applicable rates are as follows.

| Financial year | Marginal small companies' rate % | Marginal starting rate % |
|---|---|---|
| 2003 | 32.75 | 23.75 |
| 2002 | 32.75 | 23.75 |
| 2001 | 32.5 | 22.5 |
| 2000 | 32.5 | 22.5 |
| 1999 | 32.5 | — |
| 1998 | 33.5 | — |
| 1997 | 33.5 | — |

# Marginal relief

(ICTA 1988, s. 13)
Advance corporation tax rates

$$\text{Deduction} = (\text{Upper Limit} - \text{Profits}) \times \frac{\text{Basic profits}}{\text{Profits}} \times \text{Marginal Relief Fraction}$$

**'Profits'** means profits as finally computed for corporation tax purposes *plus* franked investment income *excluding* franked investment income from companies in the same group (distributions are treated as coming from within the group if the dividends so received are group income or would be group income if the companies so elected or, for distributions made on or after 6 April 1999, if the distributions are received from a company which is a 51 per cent subsidiary or a consortium company, the recipient being a member of the consortium) *plus* foreign income dividends (up to 5 April 1999).

**'Basic profits'** means profits as finally computed for corporation tax purposes (also known as 'profits chargeable to corporation tax').

Similar provisions apply for calculating marginal relief for the starting rate effective from 1 April 2000.

# Advance corporation tax rates

(Former ICTA 1988, s. 14(3))
ACT is abolished for distributions made on or after 6 April 1999 and ceases to be payable with effect from that date.

### Advance corporation tax rates

| Year | ACT rate |
|---|---|
| 1994–95 to 1998–99 (inclusive) | 1/4 |

The rate shown applies to the amount or value of the distribution, e.g. the net dividend.

Following abolition of the requirement for companies to account for ACT, there are restrictions to tax relief for surplus unutilised ACT at that date.

### Changes to dividend treatment

The *Finance (No. 2) Act* 1997 contained changes to the treatment of dividends (and other distributions on which ACT is due) affecting companies (other than charitable companies) and pension providers with effect from 2 July 1997. For dividends paid after that date, it is no longer possible to claim a payment of the associated tax credits. From 6 April 1999, entitlement to payment of tax credits disappears completely, with the sole exception of payments to non-residents under double tax treaties.

### Charge on loans to participators

(ICTA 1988, s. 419)

For loans or advances made before 6 April 1999, the rate of charge was equal to the rate of ACT for the financial year in which the loan or advance was made.

For loans or advances made on or after 6 April 1999, the rate of charge is determined by specific legislation. Under ICTA 1988, s. 419(1), this is fixed at 25 per cent of the amount of the loan or advance until further notice.

The charge itself is separate from other liabilities, being treated 'as if it were an amount of corporation tax chargeable on the company'.

# Due and payable dates

For accounting periods ending on or after 1 July 1999:

| Liability | Due date |
|---|---|
| Mainstream tax (TMA 1970, s. 59D) | Nine months and one day after end of an accounting period |
| Mainstream tax in instalments:[1]<br>• instalments | The 14th day of the seventh, tenth, 13th and 16th months after start of a 12-month accounting period |
| • balance after instalments | Nine months and one day after end of an accounting period |
| Income tax on interest, annual payments etc. | 14 days after end of return period[2] |
| Charge on loans to participators (ICTA 1988, s. 419) | Nine months and one day after the end of the accounting period in which the loan was advanced[3] |
| Advance corporation tax | 14 days after end of return period[3] |

**Notes**

[1] TMA 1970, s. 59E and SI 1998/3175 provide for the payment of corporation tax by 'large' companies (defined in accordance with the small companies' marginal relief upper limit) in instalments. The system is being phased in over a four-year period with 60 per cent, 72 per cent and 88 per cent of a large company's liability in the first, second and third year of the change being payable in instalments. Companies which are 'large' because of the number of associated companies or because of substantial dividend income will not have to pay by instalments if their corporation tax liabilities are less than £10,000 (for accounting periods ending after 30 June 2000; previously, the limit was £5,000). Companies which become 'large' in an accounting period, having previously had profits below the upper limit, may be exempt from instalment arrangements in certain circumstances. Groups containing 'large' companies are able to pay corporation tax on a group-wide basis.

[2] Return periods end on 31 March, 30 June, 30 September, 31 December and at end of accounting period. The requirement for companies to deduct and account for income tax on certain payments is removed with effect for payments after 31 March 2001 of:

• interest, royalities, annuities and other annual payments made to companies within the charge to UK corporation tax on that income; and

• interest on quoted Eurobonds paid to non-residents.

[3] ACT is abolished for distributions made on or after 6 April 1999.

# Filing deadlines

(FA 1998, Sch. 18, para. 14)

For accounting periods ending on or after 1 July 1999, the filing date for a return of profits (CT 600, or approved substitute) is generally the latest of the three dates outlined below. Note that only the first two of these are relevant unless the company is making a return in respect of an accounting period forming part of a period of account which is greater than 12 months in length.

• 12 months from the end of the return period.

• Three months after the issue of a notice to deliver a corporation tax return.

• If a period of account is greater than 12 months in length, it will be divided into two or more accounting periods.

If such a period of account is no longer than 18 months, the date for both accounting periods is 12 months from the end of the period of account.

If such a period of account is greater than 18 months, the date for the first accounting period is 30 months from the start of the period of account. The date for the second and any subsequent accounting period is 12 months from the end of that accounting period.

Notes

Obligation to file return is not automatic but is imposed by notice issued by inspector.

Where a company is not sent a notice, and has not submitted a return, it must notify the Revenue of its chargeability within 12 months of the end of the accounting period. Failure to do so can result in a penalty (see below). In any case, tax due for an accounting period should be paid by the due date. An amended return under self assessment (accounting periods ending on or after 1 July 1999) may not be made later than 12 months after the filing date stipulated above.

# Penalties

| Infringement penalised | Maximum penalty | TMA 1970 | FA 1998, Sch. 18 |
|---|---|---|---|
| Failure to notify chargeability | 100% of tax unpaid 12 months after end of accounting period | s. 10(3) | para. 2 |
| Failure to make return<br><br>• up to 3 months after filing date<br>• more than 3 months after filing date<br><br><br>• at least 18 months but less than 24 months after the end of return period<br>• 24 months or more after end of return period | *Fixed penalty*[1]<br><br>£100 (persistent failure, £500)<br><br>£200 (persistent failure, £1,000)<br>*Tax-geared penalty*[2]<br>10% of tax unpaid at 18 months after end of return period<br>20% of tax unpaid at 18 months after end of return period | s. 94(1), (5)<br><br><br><br><br><br>s. 94(6) | para. 17(2), (3)<br><br><br><br><br><br>para. 18 |
| Fraudulent or negligent submission of an incorrect return or accounts | 100% of tax lost | s. 96 | para. 20, 89 |
| Failure to keep and preserve records (subject to specific exceptions) | Up to £3,000 | – | para. 23 |
| Failure to produce documents for purposes of an enquiry | £50 plus penalty for continued failure of £30 per day (£150 per day if determined by commissioners) | – | para. 29 |

Notes

[1] Fixed-rate penalty does not apply if return filed by date allowed by Registrar of Companies.

[2] Tax-geared penalty is charged in addition to fixed penalty. Where more than one tax-geared penalty is incurred the total penalty shall not exceed the largest individual penalty on that tax.

# Interest

## Interest on overdue tax

| Interest on | Interest runs from | Provision in TMA 1970 |
|---|---|---|
| Overdue corporation tax | Date tax due and payable (nine months and one day after end of accounting period)[1] | s. 87A |
| Corporation tax payable in instalments (see p. 54) | Date instalment is due to be paid | s. 87A (as amended by SI 1998/3175) |
| Overdue income tax deducted from certain payments | 14 days after end of return period | s. 87 |
| Overdue tax due on loans to participators | Date tax due and payable | s. 109 |
| Overdue ACT[2] | 14 days after end of return period | s. 87 |

**Notes**

[1] Where one group company is liable to interest and another group company with the same accounting period is due a repayment of corporation tax an election may be made for the overpayment to be surrendered so as to reduce the interest liability of the first company which will be treated as having paid tax at the same time as the surrendering company (FA 1989, s. 102).

[2] Interest provisions cease to apply to ACT for accounting periods beginning on or after 6 April 1999 following abolition of ACT; see p. 50.

## Interest on overpaid tax

(ICTA 1988, s. 826)

Repayment interest on corporation tax runs from later of:

- due and payable date (nine months and one day after end of accounting period); and
- date of actual payment; except for
- overpayments of instalments of corporation tax (see p. 51), when interest runs from the first instalment date on which the excess amount would have been due and payable or, if later, the date on which that excess arises; and
- for companies outside the instalments regime, if tax was paid earlier than the normal due date, then interest on repayments in advance of agreement of liability runs from the first instalment date on which the excess amount would have been due and payable had the instalments regime applied or, the date on which the amount repayable was originally paid, whichever is later.

Interest on repayments of income tax deducted at source from income will run from the day after the end of the accounting period in which the income was received for accounting periods under self assessment.

# Rates of interest on overdue tax

With effect for **interest** periods commencing on 6 February 1997, the rates of interest for the purposes of late paid or unpaid corporation tax are different from those for other taxes. From that date, the rate of interest on late paid or underpaid corporation tax will depend on the accounting period for which the tax is due and, under self assessment, the nature of the tax due:

### Self assessment

For accounting periods within the self assessment regime (or CTSA – APs ending on or after 1 July 1999), these rates are distinct from those for periods before the start of self assessment because the interest is an allowable deduction for tax purposes (see below).

In addition, there are separate provisions for:

- overpaid instalments of corporation tax (which benefit from a more favourable rate – for details of payment by instalments, see below); and
- other liabilities such as the final liability due on the date specified in accordance with the table below.

### Pre-self assessment

For accounting periods before the start of self assessment, there were two rates of interest applicable to all unpaid/late paid tax depending on whether the accounting period was within the Pay and File regime (APs ending after 30 September 1993) or not (i.e. periods ending before 1 October 1993).

### CTSA (APs ending on or after 1 July 1999)
### 1. Unpaid CT (other than underpaid instalments)

| Period of application | Rate % |
|---|---|
| From 6 December 2003 | 6.50 |
| 6 August 2003 to 5 December 2003 | 5.50 |
| 6 November 2001 to 5 August 2003 | 6.50 |
| 6 May 2001 to 5 November 2001 | 7.50 |
| 6 February 2000 to 5 May 2001 | 8.50 |
| 6 March 1999 to 5 February 2000 | 7.50 |
| 6 January 1999 to 5 March 1999 | 8.50 |

## 2. Underpaid instalments

| Period of application | Rate % |
|---|---|
| From 17 November 2003 | 4.75 |
| 21 July 2003 to 16 November 2003 | 4.50 |
| 17 February 2003 to 20 July 2003 | 4.75 |
| 19 November 2001 to 16 February 2003 | 5.00 |
| 15 October 2001 to 18 November 2001 | 5.50 |
| 1 October 2001 to 14 October 2001 | 5.75 |
| 13 August 2001 to 30 September 2001 | 6.00 |
| 21 May 2001 to 12 August 2001 | 6.25 |
| 16 April 2001 to 20 May 2001 | 6.50 |
| 19 February 2001 to 15 April 2001 | 6.75 |
| 20 April 2000 to 18 February 2001 | 7.00 |
| 21 February 2000 to 19 April 2000 | 8.00 |
| 24 January 2000 to 20 February 2000 | 7.75 |
| 15 November 1999 to 23 January 2000 | 7.50 |
| 20 September 1999 to 14 November 1999 | 7.25 |
| 21 June 1999 to 19 September 1999 | 7.00 |
| 19 April 1999 to 20 June 1999 | 7.25 |
| 15 February 1999 to 18 April 1999 | 7.50 |
| 18 January 1999 to 14 February 1999 | 8.00 |

## Pre-CTSA

| Period of application | Rate % pre-Pay and File | Rate % post-Pay and File |
|---|---|---|
| From 6 December 2003 | 5.00 | 5.00 |
| 6 August 2003 to 5 December 2003 | 4.25 | 4.25 |
| 6 November 2001 to 5 August 2003 | 5.00 | 5.00 |
| 6 May 2001 to 5 November 2001 | 5.75 | 6.00 |
| 6 February 2000 to 5 May 2001 | 6.50 | 6.75 |
| 6 March 1999 to 5 February 2000 | 5.75 | 5.75 |
| 6 January 1999 to 5 March 1999 | 6.50 | 6.50 |
| 6 August 1997 to 5 January 1999 | 7.25 | 7.50 |
| 6 February 1997 to 5 August 1997 | 6.25 | 6.25 |

# Rates of interest on overpaid tax

With effect for **interest** periods commencing on 6 February 1997, the rates of interest for the purposes of overpaid corporation tax are different from those for other taxes. The rate of interest on overpaid corporation tax will depend on the accounting period for which the tax is due and, under self assessment, the nature of the tax repayable:

### Self assessment

For accounting periods within the self assessment regime (CTSA) i.e. APs on or after 1 July 1999, the rates of interest on repayments of overpaid corporation tax are distinct from those for pre-CTSA periods, because the interest is taxable (see below).

In addition, there are separate provisions for:

- overpaid instalments of corporation tax; and
- payments of corporation tax made after the normal due date.

### Pay and File and earlier periods

For accounting periods within Pay and File (APs ending after 30 September 1993) and accounting periods before Pay and File, interest on overpaid corporation tax, repayments of income tax and payments of tax credits in respect of franked investment income received is given at the appropriate rate shown in the relevant table below.

### CTSA (APs ending on or after 1 July 1999)
### 1. Overpaid CT (other than overpaid instalments and early payments of CT not due by instalments)

| Period of application | Rate % |
|---|---|
| From 6 December 2003 | 3.00 |
| 6 August 2003 to 5 December 2003 | 2.00 |
| 6 November 2001 to 5 August 2003 | 3.00 |
| 6 May 2001 to 5 November 2001 | 4.00 |
| 6 February 2000 to 5 May 2001 | 5.00 |
| 6 March 1999 to 5 February 2000 | 4.00 |
| 6 January 1999 to 5 March 1999 | 5.00 |

**2. Overpaid instalments and early payments of CT not due by instalments**

| Period of application | Rate % |
|---|---|
| From 17 November 2003 | 3.50 |
| 21 July 2003 to 16 November 2003 | 3.25 |
| 17 February 2003 to 20 July 2003 | 3.50 |
| 19 November 2001 to 16 February 2003 | 3.75 |
| 15 October 2001 to 18 November 2001 | 4.25 |
| 1 October 2001 to 14 October 2001 | 4.50 |
| 13 August 2001 to 30 September 2001 | 4.75 |
| 21 May 2001 to 12 August 2001 | 5.00 |
| 16 April 2001 to 20 May 2001 | 5.25 |
| 19 February 2001 to 15 April 2001 | 5.50 |
| 21 February 2000 to 18 February 2001 | 5.75 |
| 24 January 2000 to 20 February 2000 | 5.50 |
| 15 November 1999 to 23 January 2000 | 5.25 |
| 20 September 1999 to 14 November 1999 | 5.00 |
| 21 June 1999 to 19 September 1999 | 4.75 |
| 19 April 1999 to 20 June 1999 | 5.00 |
| 15 February 1999 to 18 April 1999 | 5.25 |
| 18 January 1999 to 14 February 1999 | 5.75 |

**Pay and File**

| Period of application | Rate % |
|---|---|
| From 6 December 2003 | 2.00 |
| 6 August 2003 to 5 December 2003 | 1.25 |
| 6 November 2001 to 5 August 2003 | 2.00 |
| 6 May 2001 to 5 November 2001 | 2.75 |
| 6 February 2000 to 5 May 2001 | 3.50 |
| 6 March 1999 to 5 February 2000 | 2.75 |
| 6 January 1999 to 5 March 1999 | 3.25 |
| 6 August 1997 to 5 January 1999 | 4.00 |
| 6 February 1996 to 5 August 1997 | 3.25 |

**Pre-Pay and File**

| Period of application | Rate % |
|---|---|
| From 6 December 2003 | 5.00 |
| 6 August 2003 to 5 December 2003 | 4.25 |
| 6 November 2001 to 5 August 2003 | 5.00 |
| 6 May 2001 to 5 November 2001 | 5.75 |
| 6 February 2000 to 5 May 2001 | 6.50 |
| 6 March 1999 to 5 February 2000 | 5.75 |
| 6 January 1999 to 5 March 1999 | 6.50 |
| 6 August 1997 to 5 January 1999 | 7.25 |
| 6 February 1996 to 5 August 1997 | 6.25 |

# Interest on overpaid/unpaid tax: income/expense

Under self-assessment interest on repayments to companies is taxable and interest payable by all companies on underpaid tax is allowable for corporation tax. They are treated as credits or debits respectively on non-trading loan relationships.

# Time limits for elections and claims

In the absence of any provision to the contrary, the normal rule is that claims are to be made within six years from the end of the relevant chargeable period (FA 1998, Sch. 18, para. 46(1) for accounting periods within self-assessment).

For details of time limits relating to payment of corporation tax, see p. 51.

In certain cases the Board *may* permit an extension of the strict time limit in relation to certain elections and claims.

| Provision | Time limit | Statutory reference |
|---|---|---|
| Stock transferred to a connected party on cessation of trade to be valued at higher of cost or sale price | 2 years from end of accounting period in which trade ceased | ICTA 1988, s. 100(1C) |
| Carry-back of ACT (from accounting periods beginning *before* 6 April 1999 only) | 2 years from end of accounting period | Former ICTA 1988, s. 239(3) |
| Surrender of ACT (from accounting periods beginning *before* 6 April 1999 only) | 6 years from end of surrendering company's accounting period | Former ICTA 1988, s. 240(1), (6) |
| Carry-forward of trading losses | Relief is given automatically | ICTA 1988, s. 393(1) |
| Set-off of trading losses against profits of the same, or an earlier, accounting period | 2 years from end of accounting period in which loss incurred (or further period allowed by Board) | ICTA 1988, s. 393A(1), (10) |
| Group relief<br><br>• where claimant company's accounting period is under self-assessment | Claims to group relief must be made (or withdrawn) by the later of:<br>(1) 12 months after the claimant company's filing date for the return for the accounting period covered by the claim;<br>(2) 30 days after the issue of a closure notice is issued on the completion of an enquiry;<br>(3) 30 days after the Revenue issue a notice of amendment to a return following the completion of an enquiry (issued where the company fails to amend the return itself); or<br>(4) 30 days after the determination of any appeal against a Revenue amendment (as in (3) above). | ICTA 1988, s. 412 and FA 1998, Sch. 18, para. 74 |

| Provision | Time limit | Statutory reference |
|---|---|---|
| | 'Enquiry' in the above does not include a restricted enquiry into an amendment to a return (restricted because the time limit for making an enquiry into the return itself has expired), where the amendment consists of a group relief claim or withdrawal of claim. | |
| | These time limits have priority over any other general time limits for amending returns and are subject to the Revenue permitting an extension to the time limits. | |
| • where claimant company's accounting period is under Pay and File | 6 years from end of claimant company's accounting period (or such longer time as the Revenue permit subject to a maximum extension of 3 months) although a claim can only be made within 2 years of the end of the accounting period where an assessment has become final | ICTA 1988, s. 412, Sch. 17A, para. 2 |
| Set-off of loss on disposal of shares in unquoted trading company against income of investment company | 2 years from end of accounting period | ICTA 1988, s. 573(2) |
| Surrender of company tax refund within group | Before refund made to surrendering company | FA 1989, s. 102(2) |
| Election for deemed transfer of capital asset to another group company prior to disposal to third party | 2 years from end of period of actual vendor in which its disposal to third party made | TCGA 1992, s. 171A |
| Notification of expenditure on plant and machinery on which capital allowances to be claimed[(1)] | 2 years from end of accounting period to which claim relates | Former FA 1994, s. 118(3) |
| Relief for non-trading deficit on loan relationships (including any non-trading exchange losses) | 2 years from end of period in which deficit arises, or, in the case of a claim to carry forward the deficit, 2 years from end of the accounting period following the deficit period, or within such further period as the Board may allow | FA 1996, s. 83(6), (7) (and as applied to exchange losses by FA 1993, s. 130(2)) |
| General claim to capital allowances under self-assessment | Claims to capital allowances must be made (or amended or withdrawn) by the later of: (1) 12 months after the claimant company's filing date for the return for the accounting period covered by the claim; | FA 1998, Sch. 18, para. 82 |

| Provision | Time limit | Statutory reference |
|---|---|---|
| | (2) 30 days after the issue of a closure notice is issued on the completion of an enquiry;<br>(3) 30 days after the Revenue issue a notice of amendment to a return following the completion of an enquiry (issued where the company fails to amend the return itself); or<br>(4) 30 days after the determination of any appeal against a Revenue amendment (as in (3) above).<br>'Enquiry' in the above does not include a restricted enquiry into an amendment to a return (restricted because the time limit for making an enquiry into the return itself has expired), where the amendment consists of a group relief claim or withdrawal of claim.<br><br>These time limits have priority over any other general time limits for amending returns and are subject to the Revenue permitting an extension to the time limits. | |
| Certain plant and machinery treated as 'short life' assets | 2 years from end of chargeable/basis period | CAA 2001, s. 85 |
| Set-off of capital allowances on special leasing | 2 years from end of accounting period | CAA 2001, s. 260(3), (6) |
| Transfer between connected parties of certain assets, eligible for capital allowances, at tax-written down value | 2 years from date of sale | CAA 2001, s. 569(1) |

# GENERAL

## Capital allowances: rates

### A. Rates of first-year allowances

| Rate (%) | Nature of expenditure | Businesses eligible to claim FYAs | When incurred | CAA 2001 |
|---|---|---|---|---|
| 100 | Certain new low-emission cars | Any | On or after 17 April 2002 and on or before 31 March 2008 | s. 45D |
| 100 | Plant and machinery used to refuel vehicles with natural gas or hydrogen fuel | Any | On or after 17 April 2002 and on or before 31 March 2008 | s. 45E |
| 100 | Expenditure on plant for use in a ring fence trade | Any company | On or after 17 April 2002 | s. 45F |
| 100 | Expenditure on designated energy-saving technologies and products | Any | On or after 1 April 2001 | s. 45A |
| 100 | Expenditure on certain ICT equipment[2] | Small[1] | On or after 1 April 2000 and on or before 31 March 2004 | s. 45 |
| 100 | Certain expenditure on machinery and plant for use primarily in Northern Ireland[3] | Small or medium sized[1] | On or after 12 May 1998 and on or before 11 May 2002 | s. 40 |
| 40 | Expenditure by on machinery and plant except long-life assets | Small or medium sized[1] | On or after 2 July 1998 | s. 45 |
| 100 | Expenditure on environmentally beneficial plant and machinery | Any | On or after 1 April 2003 | s. 45H |

**Notes**

[1] For the definition of small and medium-sized businesses, see Table B.

[2] Computers, software and internet-enabled mobile telephones.

[3] Does not apply to long-life assets, aircraft, hovercraft, certain goods vehicles and certain expenditure on assets used in agriculture, fishing or fish farming that is unapproved by the Department of Agriculture for Northern Ireland.

## B. Small and medium-sized enterprises (CAA 2001, s. 47, 49)

A company or business is a **small enterprise** if:

- it qualifies (or is treated as qualifying) as small under the *Companies Act* 1985, s. 247, for the financial year of the company in which the expenditure is incurred; and

- it is not a member of a medium or large group (*Companies Act* 1985, s. 249) at the time the expenditure is incurred.

A company or business is a **small or medium-sized enterprise if**:

- it qualifies (or is treated as qualifying) as small or medium-sized under the *Companies Act* 1985, s. 247, for the financial year of the company in which the expenditure is incurred; and

- it is not a member of a large group (*Companies Act* 1985, s. 249) at the time the expenditure is incurred.

Under the *Companies Act* 1985, s. 247, a company qualifies as small or medium-sized for a financial year if two or more of the requirements shown below are met in that and the preceding financial year. A group is small or medium-sized under the *Companies Act* 1985, s. 249 in a year in which it satisfies two or more of the requirements shown below in the relevant category.

| Type of company | Requirements | |
|---|---|---|
| Small company | Turnover | Not more than £2.8m |
| | Balance sheet total | Not more than £1.4m |
| | Number of employees | Not more than 50 |
| Medium-sized company | Turnover | Not more than £11.2m |
| | Balance sheet total | Not more than £5.6m |
| | Number of employees | Not more than 250 |
| Small group | Aggregate turnover | Not more than £2.8m net (or £3.6m gross) |
| | Aggregate balance sheet total | Not more than £1.4m net (or £1.68m gross) |
| | Aggregate number of employees | Not more than 50 |
| Medium-sized group | Aggregate turnover | Not more than £11.2m net (or £13.44m gross) |
| | Aggregate balance sheet total | Not more than £5.6m net (or £6.72m gross) |
| | Aggregate number of employees | Not more than 250 |

## Industrial buildings;[1] hotels;[2] and agricultural buildings and structures[3]

| Date of expenditure incurred | Initial allowance[4] | Writing-down allowance |
|---|---|---|
| On or after 1 November 1993 | Nil | 4% |
| 1 November 1992–31 October 1993 | 20% | 4% |
| 1 April 1986–31 October 1992 | Nil | 4% |

**Notes**

[1] The non-industrial element of an industrial building will qualify for allowances provided the cost of that element does not exceed 25% of the total cost.

[2] A qualifying hotel must provide standard hotel facilities; have at least 10 letting bedrooms and be open for at least four months between April-October, inclusive.

[3] Includes expenditure on farmhouses and buildings, cottages, fences and other works incurred for the purposes of husbandry on agricultural land (a maximum of ⅓ of expenditure on farmhouses may qualify).

## Enterprise zones:[1] industrial buildings; hotels and commercial buildings or structures[2]

| Date expenditure incurred | Initial allowance | Writing-down allowance |
|---|---|---|
| Contract to be made within 10 years of site being included within the enterprise zone (but not expenditure incurred over 20 years after the date of the site being included) | 100% | 25% |

**Notes**

[1] Areas designated by Orders made under the *Local Government, Planning and Land Act* 1980 or equivalent Northern Ireland legislation (see p. 65).

[2] Buildings or structures used for the purposes of a trade, profession or vocation (but not an industrial building or qualifying hotel) or used as offices; but not a dwelling-house.

## Flat conversion allowances[1] (CAA 2001, s. 393Aff.)

| Date expenditure incurred | Initial allowance | Writing-down allowance |
|---|---|---|
| On or after 11 May 2001 | 100% | 25% |

**Note**

[1] Expenditure on renovating or converting space above shops and other commercial premises.

## Dredging

| Date expenditure incurred | Initial allowance | Writing-down allowance |
|---|---|---|
| On or after 1 April 1986 | Nil | 4% |

## Mineral extraction[1]

| Date expenditure incurred | Initial allowance | Writing-down allowance |
|---|---|---|
| On or after 1 April 1986 | Nil | 25%[2] |

**Notes**

[1] Includes mines, oil wells and geothermal energy sources.

[2] Certain expenditure, on the acquisition of a mineral deposit and/or rights over such a deposit, qualifies for a 10% WDA.

## Research and development[1]

| Date expenditure incurred | Initial allowance | Writing-down allowance |
|---|---|---|
| On or after 5 November 1962 | 100% | No provision for WDAs |

**Note**

[1] Covers expenditure incurred for carrying out research and development, or providing facilities for such research, but not that incurred on the acquisition of rights in, or arising out of, research and development.

## Patent rights[1] and know-how[2]

| Date expenditure incurred | Initial allowance | Writing-down allowance |
|---|---|---|
| On or after 1 April 1986 | Nil | 25% |

**Notes**

[1] The purchase of patent rights includes the acquisition of a licence in respect of a patent.

[2] 'Know-how' means any industrial information and techniques likely to assist in: (i) the manufacture or processing of goods or materials; (ii) all aspects of working a mine, oil well or mineral deposit; (iii) carrying out agricultural, forestry or fishing operations.

## Dwelling houses let under assured tenancies

| Date expenditure incurred | Initial allowance | Writing-down allowance |
|---|---|---|
| 1 April 1986–31 March 1992 | Nil | 4% |

# Enterprise zones

Designated enterprise zones last for ten years from the start date and currently comprise:

| Statutory instrument | Area | Start date |
|---|---|---|
| 1993/23 | Lanarkshire (Hamilton) | 1 February 1993 |
| 1993/24 | Lanarkshire (Motherwell) | 1 February 1993 |
| 1993/25 | Lanarkshire (Monklands) | 1 February 1993 |
| 1995/2624 | Dearne Valley (Barnsley, Doncaster, Rotherham) | 3 November 1995 |
| 1995/2625 | Holmewood (North East Derbyshire) | 3 November 1995 |
| 1995/2738 | Bassetlaw | 16 November 1995 |
| 1995/2758 | Ashfield | 21 November 1995 |
| 1995/2812 | East Durham (No. 1 to No. 6) | 29 November 1995 |
| 1996/106 | Tyne Riverside (North Tyneside) | 19 February 1996 |
| 1996/1981 | Tyne Riverside (Silverlink North Scheme) | 26 August 1996 |
| 1996/1981 | Tyne Riverside (Silverlink Business Park Scheme) | 26 August 1996 |
| 1996/1981 | Tyne Riverside (Middle Engine Lane Scheme) | 26 August 1996 |
| 1996/1981 | Tyne Riverside (New York Industrial Park Scheme) | 26 August 1996 |
| 1996/1981 | Tyne Riverside (Balliol Business Park West Scheme) | 26 August 1996 |
| 1996/1981 | Tyne Riverside (Balliol Business Park East Scheme) | 26 August 1996 |
| 1996/2435 | Tyne Riverside (Baltic Enterprise Park Scheme) | 21 October 1996 |
| 1996/2435 | Tyne Riverside (Viking Industrial Park—Wagonway West Scheme) | 21 October 1996 |
| 1996/2435 | Tyne Riverside (Viking Industrial Park—Blackett Street Scheme) | 21 October 1996 |
| 1996/2435 | Tyne Riverside (Viking Industrial Park—Western Road Scheme) | 21 October 1996 |

# Lease premiums

Amount of premium assessable under Sch. A when lease granted, where duration of lease is at least one year but not more than 50 years (ICTA 1988, s. 34):

$$P \times \frac{51 - D}{50}$$

where P = total premium; and

D = duration of lease in complete years (ignoring any additional part of a year).

Amount taken into account in calculating a chargeable gain will be the balance of the premium (TCGA 1992, s. 240 and Sch. 8, para. 5, 7) for which the restriction of allowable expenditure is applicable:

| Length of lease in years | Amount chargeable as gains % | Amount within Sch. A % | Length of lease in years | Amount chargeable as gains % | Amount within Sch. A % |
|---|---|---|---|---|---|
| Over 50 | 100 | 0 | 25 | 48 | 52 |
| 50 | 98 | 2 | 24 | 46 | 54 |
| 49 | 96 | 4 | 23 | 44 | 56 |
| 48 | 94 | 6 | 22 | 42 | 58 |
| 47 | 92 | 8 | 21 | 40 | 60 |
| 46 | 90 | 10 | 20 | 38 | 62 |
| 45 | 88 | 12 | 19 | 36 | 64 |
| 44 | 86 | 14 | 18 | 34 | 66 |
| 43 | 84 | 16 | 17 | 32 | 68 |
| 42 | 82 | 18 | 16 | 30 | 70 |
| 41 | 80 | 20 | 15 | 28 | 72 |
| 40 | 78 | 22 | 14 | 26 | 74 |
| 39 | 76 | 24 | 13 | 24 | 76 |
| 38 | 74 | 26 | 12 | 22 | 78 |
| 37 | 72 | 28 | 11 | 20 | 80 |
| 36 | 70 | 30 | 10 | 18 | 82 |
| 35 | 68 | 32 | 9 | 16 | 84 |
| 34 | 66 | 34 | 8 | 14 | 86 |
| 33 | 64 | 36 | 7 | 12 | 88 |
| 32 | 62 | 38 | 6 | 10 | 90 |
| 31 | 60 | 40 | 5 | 8 | 92 |
| 30 | 58 | 42 | 4 | 6 | 94 |
| 29 | 56 | 44 | 3 | 4 | 96 |
| 28 | 54 | 46 | 2 | 2 | 98 |
| 27 | 52 | 48 | 1 or | 0 | 100 |
| 26 | 50 | 50 | less | | |

Amount of lease premium allowed as a Sch. D, Case I or II deduction:

$$\frac{\text{Schedule A charge on landlord}}{D \text{ (as above)}} \times \frac{\text{Days in accounting or basis period}}{365}$$

## Lease rentals for expensive motor cars

In respect of contracts entered into after 10 March 1992, the restricted deduction for hire charges of motor cars if the retail price was greater than £12,000 is as follows:

$$\text{Allowable amount} = \frac{£12,000 + \frac{1}{2}\,(\text{retail price} - £12,000)}{\text{retail price}} \times \text{hire charge}$$

For contracts entered into prior to 11 March 1992, the restriction applies if the retail price was greater than £8,000. The restricted deduction is as follows:

$$\text{Allowable amount} = \frac{£8,000 + \frac{1}{2}\,(\text{retail price} - £8,000)}{\text{retail price}} \times \text{hire charge}$$

## Charitable giving

### Gift Aid (FA 1990, s. 25; ICTA 1988, s. 339)

| Donations of cash by individuals and close companies to charities, etc. | Minimum qualifying cash donation[1] (net of basic rate income tax) |
|---|---|
| On or after 6 April 2000 | No minimum donation |
| 16 March 1993–5 April 2000 | £250 |

**Note**

[1] There has never been a minimum qualifying donation for non-close companies.

## Gifts of assets

| Nature of asset | Date(s) of relief | Effect of relief |
|---|---|---|
| Plant or machinery used by, or stock manufactured or sold by a trader that is given to a charity, etc. (ICTA 1988, s. 83A) | From 27 July 1999 | No disposal value brought into account as trading receipt or for capital allowances purposes |
| Plant or machinery used by, or stock manufactured or sold by, a trader that is given to a charity for medical or educational purposes for use in specific, designated countries (FA 1998, s. 47)[1] | 21 August 1998 to 26 July 1999 | No disposal value brought into account as trading receipt or for capital allowances purposes |
| Listed shares and securities, unlisted shares and securities that are dealt in on recognised stock exchanges, units in unit trusts, etc. given to a charity by an individual or company (FA 2000, s. 43) | From April 2000 | The full value of the gift is deductible when computing profits for IT or CT purposes. |
| Property settled by gift on a UK-resident trust which has a charity as beneficiary *and* the settlor retains an interest (FA 2000, s. 44) | From April 2000 | The trust income allocated to the settlor under ICTA 1988, Pt. XV will be reduced by an amount equal to the income paid to the charity in the year |

**Note**

[1] Countries are designated by Treasury Order and include those in Appendix 5 to the World Bank's 1997 Annual report (as revised from time to time) as eligible for certain funding. FA 1998, s. 47 was repealed by FA 1999, s. 55 which introduced relief under ICTA 1988, s. 83A.

# Due dates

For corporation tax, see p. 51.

For inheritance tax, see p. 115.

For value added tax, see p. 132.

For National Insurance contributions, see p. 45.

For PAYE, see p. 9.

### Income tax and capital gains tax 2004–05

Under self-assessment, tax is paid on 31 January following the year of assessment as a single sum covering capital gains tax and income tax on all sources. Interim payments on account may be required. No interim payments are required for a year of assessment if the tax paid by assessment for the preceding year was less than £500 or 20% of the total tax liability for that year. These will normally be half the amount of the net tax payable for the preceding year, but may be reduced to half the current year's liability if less. Net tax is the previous year's tax after taking off tax deducted at source and tax on dividends. For 2004–05 the following due dates apply[1]:

| First interim payment | 31 January 2005 |
|---|---|
| Second interim payment | 31 July 2005 |
| Final balancing payment | 31 January 2006 |

**Notes**

[1] If a return is not issued until after 31 October 2003 and the taxpayer has notified chargeability by 5 October 2003, the due date for the final payment becomes three months from the issue of the return (TMA 1970, s. 59B).

# Interest and surcharges

For taxation of companies, see p. 53.

For inheritance tax, see p. 105.

For value added tax, see p. 132.

### Income tax and capital gains tax 2004–05

*Interest* (TMA 1970, s. 86)

Interest is payable from the 'relevant date':

| Payment | Relevant date |
|---|---|
| First interim payment[1] | 31 January 2005 |
| Second interim payment | 31 July 2005 |
| Final payment | 31 January 2006 |
| Tax due on an amendment to a return | 31 January 2006 |
| Tax due on determination of appeal | 31 January 2006 |

**Notes**

[1] Where the taxpayer has provided the Revenue in good time with the information required to issue a statement of account ahead of the payment date of 31 January, but no statement is received before 1 January, interest on the tax to be paid will run from 30 days after the taxpayer is actually notified rather than from 31 January.

[2] Where notice to make a return is issued after 31 October 2003, then, provided there has been no failure to notify chargeability under TMA 1970, s. 7, the relevant date becomes the last day in the period of three months beginning with the day notice to make a return was given.

*Surcharges* (TMA 1970, s. 59C)

Surcharges arise as follows:

| Tax overdue | Surcharge |
|---|---|
| 28 days | 5% of tax overdue |
| 6 months | further 5% of tax overdue |

**Note**

Tax is not subject to a surcharge if it is taken into account for penalties for failure to notify – return over 12 months late or incorrect return (see p. 6). A surcharge will be repaid if one of these penalties is subsequently levied.

Surcharges apply to:

- final tax payments on self-assessments (this includes any amounts due as interim payments which remain unpaid);
- tax on inspector's amendments to a self-assessment made during or as a result of an audit;
- discovery assessments; and
- late payments of tax on assessments for 1995–96 and earlier years, where the assessment was made after 5 April 1998.

# Rates of interest on overdue income tax, capital gains tax and National Insurance contributions

The following table gives the rates of interest applicable under FA 1989, s. 178 and prescribed rates of interest (VATA 1994, s. 74 and former TMA 1970, s. 89).

| Period of application | | Rate % |
|---|---|---|
| From 6 November 2001 | | 6.50 |
| 6 May 2001 to | 5 November 2001 | 7.50 |
| 6 February 2000 to | 5 May 2001 | 8.50 |
| 6 March 1999 to | 5 February 2000 | 7.50 |
| 6 January 1999 to | 5 March 1999 | 8.50 |
| 6 August 1997 to | 5 January 1999 | 9.50 |
| 6 February 1997 to | 5 August 1997 | 8.50 |
| 6 February 1996 to | 5 February 1997 | 6.25 |

For rates applicable to companies, see p. 54.

## Rates of interest on income tax, capital gains tax and National Insurance contributions repayments

Interest on tax repayments qualifying for repayment supplement is given at the following rates.

| Date | | Rate % |
|---|---|---|
| From 6 November 2001 | | 2.50 |
| 6 May 2001 to | 5 November 2001 | 3.50 |
| 6 February 2000 to | 5 May 2001 | 4.00 |
| 6 March 1999 to | 5 February 2000 | 3.00 |
| 6 January 1999 to | 5 March 1999 | 4.00 |
| 6 August 1997 to | 5 January 1999 | 4.75 |
| 6 February 1997 to | 5 August 1997 | 4.00 |
| 6 February 1996 to | 5 February 1997 | 6.25 |

**Notes**

The qualifying period is as set out below: **For individuals:** From the date of payment (deemed to be 31 January following the tax year in respect of tax deducted at source) to the date on which the order for the repayment is issued. For periods prior to self-assessment, the qualifying period was the later of:

(i)   the due date; or

(ii)  the actual date of payment,

until the end of the tax month in which the repayment order is issued. The *Finance Act* 1997 contained provision for interest on repayments of overpaid tax to run from the date on which tax is paid – even if this is earlier than the due date.

## Certificates of tax deposit (CTDs)

The interest rates that follow apply to CTDs issued under the Series 7 prospectus.

CTDs (Series 7) can be purchased to settle most tax liabilities, except PAYE, VAT and corporation tax falling due under Pay and File, or for subsequent encashment. (No CTDs are available for purchase for use against corporation tax liabilities since the start of the Pay and File regime.) A higher rate of interest is paid if the CTD is used in payment of tax. Interest is allowed/paid gross and is taxable.

Rates of interest vary according to the period for which the deposit is held. The rates in force at issue apply for one year; thereafter the rate applicable is that on the most recent anniversary of the date of issue.

Deposits must be maintained at £2,000 or over. A deposit of less than £100,000 can be made at any tax collection office. Larger deposits must be sent to the Bank of England (Drawing Office) (for the General Account of the Commissioners of Inland Revenue, No. 23411007) with a confirmatory letter to the Central Accounting Office (CTD), Inland Revenue (A), Barrington Road, Worthing, West Sussex, BN12 4XH.

Copies of the Series 7 prospectus, giving full details concerning CTDs, can be obtained from any collection office or the Central Accounting Office.

Rates applicable over recent years have been as follows:

# Certificates of tax deposit (Series 7): rates of interest

| Deposits on or after | Deposits under £100,000 | | Deposits of £100,000 or more | | | | | | | | | |
| --- | --- | --- | --- | --- | --- | --- | --- | --- | --- | --- | --- | --- |
| | | | Deposits held for under 1 month | | Deposits held for 1 to under 3 months | | Deposits held for 3 to under 6 months | | Deposits held for 6 to under 9 months | | Deposits held for 9–12 months | |
| | Applied in payment of tax % | Cash value % | Applied in payment of tax % | Cash value % | Applied in payment of tax % | Cash value % | Applied in payment of tax % | Cash value % | Applied in payment of tax % | Cash value % | Applied in payment of tax % | Cash value % |
| 11 Mar. 1996 | 2.50 | 1.25 | 2.50 | 1.25 | 5 | 2.50 | 4.75 | 2.50 | 4.75 | 2.50 | 4.25 | 2.25 |
| 7 June 1996 | 2.25 | 1.25 | 2.25 | 1.50 | 4.75 | 2.50 | 4.75 | 2.50 | 4.75 | 2.50 | 4.75 | 2.50 |
| 31 Oct. 1996 | 2.50 | 1.25 | 2.50 | 1.25 | 5.25 | 2.75 | 5 | 2.50 | 5 | 2.50 | 5 | 2.50 |
| 7 May 1997 | 2.75 | 1.50 | 2.75 | 1.50 | 5.50 | 2.75 | 5.25 | 2.75 | 5.50 | 2.75 | 5.25 | 2.75 |
| 9 June 1997 | 3 | 1.50 | 3 | 1.50 | 5.50 | 2.75 | 5.50 | 2.75 | 5.50 | 2.75 | 5.50 | 2.75 |
| 11 July 1997 | 3.25 | 1.75 | 3.25 | 1.75 | 6 | 3 | 5.75 | 3 | 5.75 | 3 | 6 | 3 |
| 8 Aug. 1997 | 4.50 | 2.25 | 4.50 | 2.25 | 6 | 3 | 6 | 3 | 6 | 3 | 6 | 3 |
| 7 Nov. 1997 | 4 | 2 | 4 | 2 | 6.50 | 3.25 | 6.50 | 3.25 | 6.25 | 3.25 | 5.75 | 3.25 |
| 5 June 1998 | 4 | 2 | 4 | 2 | 6.50 | 3.25 | 6.25 | 3.25 | 6.25 | 3.25 | 6 | 3 |
| 9 Oct. 1998 | 3.75 | 2 | 3.75 | 2 | 6.25 | 3.25 | 5.75 | 3 | 5.50 | 2.75 | 5.25 | 2.75 |
| 6 Nov. 1998 | 3.25 | 1.75 | 3.25 | 1.75 | 5.75 | 3 | 5.25 | 2.75 | 5 | 2.50 | 4.75 | 2.50 |
| 5 Feb. 1999 | 1.75 | 1 | 1.75 | 1 | 4.50 | 2.25 | 4 | 2 | 3.75 | 2 | 3.75 | 2 |
| 9 Apr. 1999 | 1.75 | 1 | 1.75 | 1 | 4.50 | 2 | 4 | 2 | 3.75 | 2 | 3.75 | 2 |
| 11 June 1999 | 1.50 | 0.75 | 1.50 | 0.75 | 4 | 2 | 4 | 2 | 4 | 2 | 4 | 2 |
| 9 Sept. 1999 | 1.75 | 1 | 1.75 | 1 | 4.50 | 2.25 | 4.50 | 2.25 | 4.50 | 2.25 | 4.50 | 2.25 |
| 4 Nov. 1999 | 2 | 1 | 2 | 1 | 5 | 2.50 | 4.75 | 2.50 | 4.75 | 2.50 | 4.75 | 2.50 |
| 14 Jan. 2000 | 2.25 | 1.25 | 2.25 | 1.25 | 5 | 2.50 | 5 | 2.50 | 5 | 2.50 | 5.25 | 2.50 |
| 11 Feb. 2000 | 2.50 | 1.25 | 2.50 | 1.25 | 5.25 | 2.75 | 5 | 2.50 | 5.25 | 2.75 | 5.25 | 2.75 |
| 9 Feb. 2001 | 2.25 | 1.25 | 2.25 | 1.25 | 4.75 | 2.50 | 4.25 | 2.25 | 4.25 | 2.25 | 4 | 2 |
| 6 Apr. 2001 | 2 | 1 | 2 | 1 | 4.25 | 2.25 | 4 | 2 | 3.75 | 2 | 3.50 | 1.75 |
| 11 May 2001 | 2 | 1 | 2 | 1 | 4 | 2 | 4 | 2 | 3.75 | 2 | 3.75 | 2 |
| 3 Aug. 2001 | 1.50 | 0.75 | 1.50 | 0.75 | 4 | 2 | 3.75 | 1.875 | 3.75 | 1.875 | 3.75 | 1.875 |
| 5 Oct. 2001 | 1 | 0.50 | 1 | 0.50 | 3.25 | 1.75 | 3 | 1.50 | 3 | 1.50 | 3 | 1.50 |
| 9 Nov. 2001 | 0.50 | 0.25 | 0.50 | 0.25 | 2.75 | 1.50 | 2.50 | 1.25 | 2.25 | 1.25 | 2.25 | 1.25 |
| 7 Feb. 2003 | 0.25 | 0.00 | 0.25 | 0.00 | 2.75 | 1.25 | 2.25 | 1.00 | 2.25 | 1.00 | 2.00 | 1.00 |
| 11 July 2003 | 0.00 | 0.00 | 0.00 | 0.00 | 2.50 | 1.25 | 2.25 | 1.00 | 2.00 | 1.00 | 2.00 | 1.00 |
| 7 Nov. 2003 | 0.25 | 0.00 | 0.25 | 0.00 | 3.00 | 1.50 | 3.00 | 1.50 | 3.00 | 1.50 | 3.00 | 1.50 |

# Remission of tax for official error
(ESC A19)

Under ESC A19, arrears of income tax and capital gains tax may be given up if they result from the Revenue's failure to make proper and timely use of information supplied by the taxpayer, or in certain circumstances by the taxpayer's employer or the Department for Work and Pensions.

The taxpayer must have reasonably believed that his or her affairs were in order. Tax will normally only be given up where there was a gap of 12 months or more between the Revenue receiving the information that tax was due, and notifying the taxpayer of the arrears.

# Retail prices index

The retail prices index (RPI) issued by the Department of Employment is used to calculate the indexation allowance for capital gains tax purposes. Certain personal and other reliefs are also linked to the RPI, subject to Parliament determining otherwise.

With effect from February 1987 the reference date to which the price level in each subsequent month is related was changed from 'January 1974 = 100' to 'January 1987 = 100' (with a base of January 1974 = 100, January 1987's RPI was 394.5). Movements in the RPI in the months after January 1987 are calculated with reference to January 1987 = 100. A new formula has been provided by the Department of Employment for calculating movements in the index over periods which span January 1987:

> "The index for the later month (January 1987 = 100) is multiplied by the index for January 1987 (January 1974 = 100) and divided by the index for the earlier month (January 1974 = 100). 100 is subtracted to give the percentage change between the two months."

CCH has prepared the following table in accordance with this formula:

|  | 1982 | 1983 | 1984 | 1985 | 1986 | 1987 | 1988 | 1989 | 1990 | 1991 | 1992 |
|---|---|---|---|---|---|---|---|---|---|---|---|
| January |  | 82.61 | 86.84 | 91.20 | 96.25 | 100.0 | 103.3 | 111.0 | 119.5 | 130.2 | 135.6 |
| February |  | 82.97 | 87.20 | 91.94 | 96.60 | 100.4 | 103.7 | 111.8 | 120.2 | 130.9 | 136.3 |
| March | 79.44 | 83.12 | 87.48 | 92.80 | 96.73 | 100.6 | 104.1 | 112.3 | 121.4 | 131.4 | 136.7 |
| April | 81.04 | 84.28 | 88.64 | 94.78 | 97.67 | 101.8 | 105.8 | 114.3 | 125.1 | 133.1 | 138.8 |
| May | 81.62 | 84.64 | 88.97 | 95.21 | 97.85 | 101.9 | 106.2 | 115.0 | 126.2 | 133.5 | 139.3 |
| June | 81.85 | 84.84 | 89.20 | 95.41 | 97.79 | 101.9 | 106.6 | 115.4 | 126.7 | 134.1 | 139.3 |
| July | 81.88 | 85.30 | 89.10 | 95.23 | 97.52 | 101.8 | 106.7 | 115.5 | 126.8 | 133.8 | 138.8 |
| August | 81.90 | 85.68 | 89.94 | 95.49 | 97.82 | 102.1 | 107.9 | 115.8 | 128.1 | 134.1 | 138.9 |
| September | 81.85 | 86.06 | 90.11 | 95.44 | 98.30 | 102.4 | 108.4 | 116.6 | 129.3 | 134.6 | 139.4 |
| October | 82.26 | 86.36 | 90.67 | 95.59 | 98.45 | 102.9 | 109.5 | 117.5 | 130.3 | 135.1 | 139.9 |
| November | 82.66 | 86.67 | 90.95 | 95.92 | 99.29 | 103.4 | 110.0 | 118.5 | 130.0 | 135.6 | 139.7 |
| December | 82.51 | 86.89 | 90.87 | 96.05 | 99.62 | 103.3 | 110.3 | 118.8 | 129.9 | 135.7 | 139.2 |

|  | 1993 | 1994 | 1995 | 1996 | 1997 | 1998 | 1999 | 2000 | 2001 | 2002 | 2003 |
|---|---|---|---|---|---|---|---|---|---|---|---|
| January | 137.9 | 141.3 | 146.0 | 150.2 | 154.4 | 159.5 | 163.4 | 166.6 | 171.1 | 173.3 | 178.4 |
| February | 138.8 | 142.1 | 146.9 | 150.9 | 155.0 | 160.3 | 163.7 | 167.5 | 172.0 | 173.8 | 179.3 |
| March | 139.3 | 142.5 | 147.5 | 151.5 | 155.4 | 160.8 | 164.1 | 168.4 | 172.2 | 174.5 | 179.9 |
| April | 140.6 | 144.2 | 149.0 | 152.6 | 156.3 | 162.6 | 165.2 | 170.1 | 173.1 | 175.7 | 181.2 |
| May | 141.1 | 144.7 | 149.6 | 152.9 | 156.9 | 163.5 | 165.6 | 170.7 | 174.2 | 176.2 | 181.5 |
| June | 141.0 | 144.7 | 149.8 | 153.0 | 157.5 | 163.4 | 165.6 | 171.1 | 174.4 | 176.2 | 181.3 |
| July | 140.7 | 144.0 | 149.1 | 152.4 | 157.5 | 163.0 | 165.1 | 170.5 | 173.3 | 175.9 | 181.3 |
| August | 141.3 | 144.7 | 149.9 | 153.1 | 158.5 | 163.7 | 165.5 | 170.5 | 174.0 | 176.4 | 181.6 |
| September | 141.9 | 145.0 | 150.6 | 153.8 | 159.3 | 164.4 | 166.2 | 171.7 | 174.6 | 177.6 | 182.5 |
| October | 141.8 | 145.2 | 149.8 | 153.8 | 159.5 | 164.5 | 166.5 | 171.6 | 174.3 | 177.9 | 182.6 |
| November | 141.6 | 145.3 | 149.8 | 153.9 | 159.6 | 164.4 | 166.7 | 172.1 | 173.6 | 178.2 |  |
| December | 141.9 | 146.0 | 150.7 | 154.4 | 160.0 | 164.4 | 167.3 | 172.2 | 173.4 | 178.5 |  |

Tables showing the indexed rise concerning recent disposals follow.

# RD month (October 2002–October 2003) January 1987 = 100

| RI Month | 2002 Oct. | Nov. | Dec. | 2003 Jan. | Feb. | Mar. | April | May | June | July | Aug. | Sept. | Oct. |
|---|---|---|---|---|---|---|---|---|---|---|---|---|
| **1982** March | 1.239 | 1.243 | 1.247 | 1.246 | 1.257 | 1.265 | 1.281 | 1.285 | 1.282 | 1.282 | 1.286 | 1.297 | 1.299 |
| April | 1.195 | 1.199 | 1.203 | 1.201 | 1.213 | 1.220 | 1.236 | 1.240 | 1.237 | 1.237 | 1.241 | 1.252 | 1.253 |
| May | 1.180 | 1.183 | 1.187 | 1.186 | 1.197 | 1.204 | 1.220 | 1.224 | 1.221 | 1.221 | 1.225 | 1.236 | 1.237 |
| June | 1.173 | 1.177 | 1.181 | 1.180 | 1.191 | 1.198 | 1.214 | 1.217 | 1.215 | 1.215 | 1.219 | 1.230 | 1.231 |
| July | 1.173 | 1.176 | 1.180 | 1.179 | 1.190 | 1.197 | 1.213 | 1.217 | 1.214 | 1.214 | 1.218 | 1.229 | 1.230 |
| Aug. | 1.172 | 1.176 | 1.179 | 1.178 | 1.189 | 1.197 | 1.212 | 1.216 | 1.214 | 1.214 | 1.217 | 1.228 | 1.230 |
| Sept. | 1.173 | 1.177 | 1.181 | 1.180 | 1.191 | 1.198 | 1.214 | 1.217 | 1.215 | 1.215 | 1.219 | 1.230 | 1.231 |
| Oct. | 1.163 | 1.166 | 1.170 | 1.169 | 1.180 | 1.187 | 1.203 | 1.207 | 1.204 | 1.204 | 1.208 | 1.219 | 1.220 |
| Nov. | 1.152 | 1.156 | 1.159 | 1.158 | 1.169 | 1.176 | 1.192 | 1.196 | 1.193 | 1.193 | 1.197 | 1.208 | 1.209 |
| Dec. | 1.156 | 1.160 | 1.163 | 1.162 | 1.173 | 1.180 | 1.196 | 1.200 | 1.197 | 1.197 | 1.201 | 1.212 | 1.213 |
| **1983** Jan. | 1.153 | 1.157 | 1.161 | 1.160 | 1.170 | 1.178 | 1.193 | 1.197 | 1.195 | 1.195 | 1.198 | 1.209 | 1.210 |
| Feb. | 1.144 | 1.148 | 1.151 | 1.150 | 1.161 | 1.168 | 1.184 | 1.188 | 1.185 | 1.185 | 1.189 | 1.200 | 1.201 |
| March | 1.140 | 1.144 | 1.148 | 1.146 | 1.157 | 1.164 | 1.180 | 1.184 | 1.181 | 1.181 | 1.185 | 1.196 | 1.197 |
| April | 1.111 | 1.114 | 1.118 | 1.117 | 1.127 | 1.134 | 1.150 | 1.153 | 1.151 | 1.151 | 1.155 | 1.165 | 1.166 |
| May | 1.102 | 1.105 | 1.109 | 1.108 | 1.118 | 1.126 | 1.141 | 1.144 | 1.142 | 1.142 | 1.146 | 1.156 | 1.157 |
| June | 1.097 | 1.100 | 1.104 | 1.103 | 1.113 | 1.120 | 1.136 | 1.139 | 1.137 | 1.137 | 1.140 | 1.151 | 1.152 |
| July | 1.086 | 1.089 | 1.093 | 1.091 | 1.102 | 1.109 | 1.124 | 1.128 | 1.125 | 1.125 | 1.129 | 1.140 | 1.141 |
| Aug. | 1.076 | 1.080 | 1.083 | 1.082 | 1.093 | 1.100 | 1.115 | 1.118 | 1.116 | 1.116 | 1.120 | 1.130 | 1.131 |
| Sept. | 1.067 | 1.071 | 1.074 | 1.073 | 1.083 | 1.090 | 1.106 | 1.109 | 1.107 | 1.107 | 1.110 | 1.121 | 1.122 |
| Oct. | 1.060 | 1.063 | 1.067 | 1.066 | 1.076 | 1.083 | 1.098 | 1.102 | 1.102 | 1.099 | 1.099 | 1.113 | 1.114 |
| Nov. | 1.053 | 1.056 | 1.060 | 1.058 | 1.069 | 1.076 | 1.091 | 1.094 | 1.092 | 1.092 | 1.095 | 1.106 | 1.107 |
| Dec. | 1.047 | 1.051 | 1.054 | 1.053 | 1.063 | 1.070 | 1.085 | 1.089 | 1.086 | 1.086 | 1.090 | 1.100 | 1.101 |
| **1984** Jan. | 1.048 | 1.052 | 1.055 | 1.054 | 1.065 | 1.072 | 1.086 | 1.090 | 1.088 | 1.088 | 1.091 | 1.101 | 1.103 |
| Feb. | 1.404 | 1.044 | 1.047 | 1.046 | 1.056 | 1.063 | 1.078 | 1.081 | 1.079 | 1.079 | 1.083 | 1.093 | 1.094 |
| March | 1.034 | 1.037 | 1.041 | 1.039 | 1.050 | 1.057 | 1.071 | 1.075 | 1.073 | 1.073 | 1.076 | 1.086 | 1.087 |
| April | 1.007 | 1.010 | 1.014 | 1.013 | 1.023 | 1.029 | 1.044 | 1.048 | 1.045 | 1.045 | 1.049 | 1.059 | 1.060 |
| May | 0.999 | 1.003 | 1.006 | 1.005 | 1.015 | 1.022 | 1.037 | 1.040 | 1.038 | 1.038 | 1.041 | 1.051 | 1.052 |
| June | 0.994 | 0.998 | 1.001 | 1.000 | 1.010 | 1.017 | 1.031 | 1.035 | 1.032 | 1.032 | 1.036 | 1.046 | 1.047 |
| July | 0.997 | 1.000 | 1.003 | 1.002 | 1.012 | 1.019 | 1.034 | 1.037 | 1.035 | 1.035 | 1.038 | 1.048 | 1.049 |
| Aug. | 0.978 | 0.981 | 0.985 | 0.984 | 0.994 | 1.000 | 1.015 | 1.018 | 1.016 | 1.016 | 1.019 | 1.029 | 1.030 |
| Sept. | 0.974 | 0.977 | 0.981 | 0.980 | 0.990 | 0.996 | 1.011 | 1.014 | 1.012 | 1.012 | 1.015 | 1.025 | 1.026 |
| Oct. | 0.962 | 0.965 | 0.969 | 0.968 | 0.997 | 0.984 | 0.998 | 1.002 | 1.000 | 1.000 | 1.003 | 1.013 | 1.014 |
| Nov. | 0.956 | 0.959 | 0.963 | 0.962 | 0.971 | 0.978 | 0.992 | 0.996 | 0.993 | 0.993 | 0.997 | 1.007 | 1.008 |
| Dec. | 0.958 | 0.961 | 0.964 | 0.963 | 0.973 | 0.980 | 0.994 | 0.997 | 0.995 | 0.995 | 0.998 | 1.008 | 1.009 |

| RI Month | 2002 | | | 2003 | | | | | | | | | |
|---|---|---|---|---|---|---|---|---|---|---|---|---|---|
| | Oct. | Nov. | Dec. | Jan. | Feb. | Mar. | April | May | June | July | Aug. | Sept. | Oct. |
| **1985** Jan. | 0.951 | 0.954 | 0.957 | 0.956 | 0.966 | 0.973 | 0.987 | 0.990 | 0.998 | 0.998 | 0.991 | 1.001 | 1.002 |
| Feb. | 0.935 | 0.938 | 0.942 | 0.940 | 0.950 | 0.957 | 0.971 | 0.974 | 0.972 | 0.972 | 0.975 | 0.985 | 0.986 |
| March | 0.917 | 0.920 | 0.923 | 0.922 | 0.932 | 0.939 | 0.953 | 0.956 | 0.954 | 0.954 | 0.957 | 0.967 | 0.968 |
| April | 0.877 | 0.880 | 0.883 | 0.882 | 0.892 | 0.898 | 0.912 | 0.915 | 0.913 | 0.913 | 0.916 | 0.926 | 0.927 |
| May | 0.869 | 0.872 | 0.875 | 0.874 | 0.883 | 0.890 | 0.903 | 0.906 | 0.904 | 0.904 | 0.907 | 0.917 | 0.918 |
| June | 0.865 | 0.868 | 0.871 | 0.870 | 0.879 | 0.886 | 0.899 | 0.902 | 0.900 | 0.900 | 0.903 | 0.913 | 0.914 |
| July | 0.868 | 0.871 | 0.874 | 0.873 | 0.883 | 0.889 | 0.903 | 0.906 | 0.904 | 0.904 | 0.907 | 0.916 | 0.917 |
| Aug. | 0.863 | 0.866 | 0.869 | 0.868 | 0.878 | 0.884 | 0.898 | 0.901 | 0.899 | 0.899 | 0.902 | 0.911 | 0.912 |
| Sept. | 0.864 | 0.867 | 0.870 | 0.869 | 0.879 | 0.885 | 0.899 | 0.902 | 0.900 | 0.900 | 0.903 | 0.912 | 0.913 |
| Oct. | 0.861 | 0.864 | 0.867 | 0.866 | 0.876 | 0.882 | 0.896 | 0.899 | 0.897 | 0.897 | 0.900 | 0.909 | 0.910 |
| Nov. | 0.855 | 0.858 | 0.861 | 0.860 | 0.869 | 0.876 | 0.889 | 0.892 | 0.890 | 0.890 | 0.893 | 0.903 | 0.904 |
| Dec. | 0.852 | 0.855 | 0.858 | 0.857 | 0.867 | 0.873 | 0.887 | 0.890 | 0.888 | 0.888 | 0.891 | 0.900 | 0.901 |
| **1986** Jan. | 0.848 | 0.851 | 0.855 | 0.854 | 0.863 | 0.869 | 0.883 | 0.886 | 0.884 | 0.884 | 0.887 | 0.896 | 0.897 |
| Feb. | 0.842 | 0.845 | 0.848 | 0.847 | 0.856 | 0.862 | 0.876 | 0.879 | 0.877 | 0.877 | 0.880 | 0.889 | 0.890 |
| March | 0.839 | 0.842 | 0.845 | 0.844 | 0.854 | 0.860 | 0.873 | 0.876 | 0.874 | 0.874 | 0.877 | 0.887 | 0.888 |
| April | 0.821 | 0.825 | 0.828 | 0.827 | 0.836 | 0.842 | 0.855 | 0.858 | 0.856 | 0.856 | 0.859 | 0.869 | 0.870 |
| May | 0.818 | 0.821 | 0.824 | 0.823 | 0.832 | 0.839 | 0.852 | 0.855 | 0.853 | 0.853 | 0.856 | 0.865 | 0.866 |
| June | 0.819 | 0.822 | 0.825 | 0.824 | 0.833 | 0.840 | 0.853 | 0.856 | 0.854 | 0.854 | 0.857 | 0.866 | 0.867 |
| July | 0.824 | 0.827 | 0.830 | 0.829 | 0.839 | 0.845 | 0.858 | 0.861 | 0.859 | 0.859 | 0.862 | 0.871 | 0.873 |
| Aug. | 0.819 | 0.822 | 0.825 | 0.824 | 0.833 | 0.839 | 0.852 | 0.855 | 0.853 | 0.853 | 0.856 | 0.866 | 0.867 |
| Sept. | 0.810 | 0.813 | 0.816 | 0.815 | 0.824 | 0.830 | 0.843 | 0.846 | 0.844 | 0.844 | 0.847 | 0.857 | 0.858 |
| Oct. | 0.807 | 0.810 | 0.813 | 0.812 | 0.821 | 0.827 | 0.840 | 0.844 | 0.841 | 0.841 | 0.845 | 0.854 | 0.855 |
| Nov. | 0.792 | 0.795 | 0.798 | 0.797 | 0.806 | 0.812 | 0.825 | 0.828 | 0.826 | 0.826 | 0.829 | 0.838 | 0.839 |
| Dec. | 0.786 | 0.789 | 0.792 | 0.791 | 0.800 | 0.806 | 0.819 | 0.822 | 0.820 | 0.820 | 0.823 | 0.832 | 0.833 |
| **1987** Jan. | 0.779 | 0.782 | 0.785 | 0.784 | 0.793 | 0.799 | 0.812 | 0.815 | 0.813 | 0.813 | 0.816 | 0.825 | 0.826 |
| Feb. | 0.772 | 0.775 | 0.778 | 0.777 | 0.786 | 0.792 | 0.805 | 0.808 | 0.806 | 0.806 | 0.809 | 0.818 | 0.819 |
| March | 0.768 | 0.771 | 0.774 | 0.773 | 0.782 | 0.788 | 0.801 | 0.804 | 0.802 | 0.802 | 0.805 | 0.814 | 0.815 |
| April | 0.748 | 0.750 | 0.753 | 0.752 | 0.761 | 0.767 | 0.780 | 0.783 | 0.781 | 0.781 | 0.784 | 0.793 | 0.794 |
| May | 0.746 | 0.749 | 0.752 | 0.751 | 0.760 | 0.765 | 0.778 | 0.781 | 0.779 | 0.779 | 0.782 | 0.791 | 0.792 |
| June | 0.746 | 0.749 | 0.752 | 0.751 | 0.760 | 0.765 | 0.778 | 0.781 | 0.779 | 0.779 | 0.782 | 0.791 | 0.792 |
| July | 0.748 | 0.750 | 0.753 | 0.752 | 0.761 | 0.767 | 0.780 | 0.783 | 0.781 | 0.781 | 0.784 | 0.793 | 0.794 |
| Aug. | 0.742 | 0.745 | 0.748 | 0.747 | 0.756 | 0.762 | 0.775 | 0.778 | 0.776 | 0.776 | 0.779 | 0.787 | 0.788 |
| Sept. | 0.737 | 0.740 | 0.743 | 0.742 | 0.751 | 0.757 | 0.770 | 0.772 | 0.771 | 0.771 | 0.773 | 0.782 | 0.783 |
| Oct. | 0.729 | 0.732 | 0.735 | 0.734 | 0.742 | 0.748 | 0.761 | 0.764 | 0.762 | 0.762 | 0.765 | 0.774 | 0.775 |
| Nov. | 0.721 | 0.723 | 0.726 | 0.725 | 0.734 | 0.740 | 0.752 | 0.755 | 0.753 | 0.753 | 0.756 | 0.765 | 0.766 |
| Dec. | 0.722 | 0.725 | 0.728 | 0.727 | 0.736 | 0.742 | 0.754 | 0.757 | 0.755 | 0.755 | 0.758 | 0.767 | 0.768 |

| RI Month | 2002 Oct. | Nov. | Dec. | 2003 Jan. | Feb. | Mar. | April | May | June | July | Aug. | Sept. | Oct. |
|---|---|---|---|---|---|---|---|---|---|---|---|---|---|
| **1988** Jan. | 0.722 | 0.725 | 0.728 | 0.727 | 0.736 | 0.742 | 0.754 | 0.757 | 0.755 | 0.755 | 0.758 | 0.767 | 0.768 |
| Feb. | 0.716 | 0.718 | 0.721 | 0.720 | 0.729 | 0.735 | 0.747 | 0.750 | 0.748 | 0.748 | 0.751 | 0.760 | 0.761 |
| March | 0.709 | 0.712 | 0.715 | 0.714 | 0.722 | 0.728 | 0.741 | 0.744 | 0.742 | 0.742 | 0.744 | 0.753 | 0.754 |
| April | 0.681 | 0.684 | 0.687 | 0.686 | 0.695 | 0.700 | 0.713 | 0.716 | 0.714 | 0.714 | 0.716 | 0.725 | 0.726 |
| May | 0.675 | 0.678 | 0.681 | 0.680 | 0.688 | 0.694 | 0.706 | 0.709 | 0.707 | 0.707 | 0.710 | 0.718 | 0.719 |
| June | 0.669 | 0.672 | 0.674 | 0.674 | 0.682 | 0.688 | 0.700 | 0.703 | 0.701 | 0.701 | 0.704 | 0.712 | 0.713 |
| July | 0.667 | 0.670 | 0.673 | 0.672 | 0.680 | 0.686 | 0.698 | 0.701 | 0.699 | 0.699 | 0.702 | 0.710 | 0.711 |
| Aug. | 0.649 | 0.652 | 0.654 | 0.653 | 0.662 | 0.667 | 0.679 | 0.682 | 0.680 | 0.680 | 0.683 | 0.691 | 0.692 |
| Sept. | 0.641 | 0.644 | 0.647 | 0.646 | 0.654 | 0.660 | 0.672 | 0.674 | 0.673 | 0.673 | 0.675 | 0.684 | 0.685 |
| Oct. | 0.625 | 0.627 | 0.630 | 0.629 | 0.637 | 0.643 | 0.655 | 0.658 | 0.656 | 0.656 | 0.658 | 0.667 | 0.668 |
| Nov. | 0.617 | 0.620 | 0.623 | 0.622 | 0.630 | 0.635 | 0.647 | 0.650 | 0.648 | 0.648 | 0.651 | 0.659 | 0.660 |
| Dec. | 0.613 | 0.616 | 0.618 | 0.617 | 0.626 | 0.631 | 0.643 | 0.646 | 0.644 | 0.644 | 0.646 | 0.655 | 0.655 |
| **1989** Jan. | 0.603 | 0.605 | 0.608 | 0.607 | 0.615 | 0.621 | 0.632 | 0.635 | 0.633 | 0.633 | 0.636 | 0.644 | 0.645 |
| Feb. | 0.591 | 0.594 | 0.597 | 0.596 | 0.604 | 0.609 | 0.621 | 0.623 | 0.622 | 0.622 | 0.624 | 0.632 | 0.633 |
| March | 0.584 | 0.587 | 0.589 | 0.589 | 0.597 | 0.602 | 0.614 | 0.616 | 0.614 | 0.614 | 0.617 | 0.625 | 0.626 |
| April | 0.556 | 0.559 | 0.562 | 0.561 | 0.569 | 0.574 | 0.585 | 0.588 | 0.586 | 0.586 | 0.589 | 0.597 | 0.598 |
| May | 0.547 | 0.550 | 0.552 | 0.551 | 0.559 | 0.564 | 0.576 | 0.578 | 0.577 | 0.577 | 0.579 | 0.587 | 0.588 |
| June | 0.542 | 0.544 | 0.547 | 0.546 | 0.554 | 0.559 | 0.570 | 0.573 | 0.571 | 0.571 | 0.574 | 0.581 | 0.582 |
| July | 0.540 | 0.543 | 0.545 | 0.545 | 0.552 | 0.558 | 0.569 | 0.571 | 0.570 | 0.570 | 0.572 | 0.580 | 0.581 |
| Aug. | 0.536 | 0.539 | 0.541 | 0.541 | 0.548 | 0.554 | 0.565 | 0.567 | 0.566 | 0.566 | 0.568 | 0.576 | 0.577 |
| Sept. | 0.526 | 0.528 | 0.531 | 0.530 | 0.538 | 0.543 | 0.554 | 0.557 | 0.555 | 0.555 | 0.557 | 0.565 | 0.566 |
| Oct. | 0.514 | 0.517 | 0.519 | 0.518 | 0.526 | 0.531 | 0.542 | 0.545 | 0.543 | 0.543 | 0.546 | 0.553 | 0.554 |
| Nov. | 0.501 | 0.504 | 0.506 | 0.505 | 0.513 | 0.518 | 0.529 | 0.532 | 0.530 | 0.530 | 0.532 | 0.540 | 0.541 |
| Dec. | 0.497 | 0.500 | 0.503 | 0.502 | 0.509 | 0.514 | 0.525 | 0.528 | 0.526 | 0.526 | 0.529 | 0.536 | 0.537 |
| **1990** Jan. | 0.489 | 0.491 | 0.494 | 0.493 | 0.500 | 0.505 | 0.516 | 0.519 | 0.517 | 0.517 | 0.520 | 0.527 | 0.528 |
| Feb. | 0.480 | 0.483 | 0.485 | 0.484 | 0.492 | 0.497 | 0.507 | 0.510 | 0.508 | 0.508 | 0.511 | 0.518 | 0.519 |
| March | 0.465 | 0.468 | 0.470 | 0.470 | 0.477 | 0.482 | 0.493 | 0.495 | 0.493 | 0.493 | 0.496 | 0.503 | 0.504 |
| April | 0.422 | 0.424 | 0.427 | 0.426 | 0.433 | 0.438 | 0.448 | 0.451 | 0.449 | 0.449 | 0.452 | 0.459 | 0.460 |
| May | 0.410 | 0.412 | 0.414 | 0.414 | 0.421 | 0.426 | 0.436 | 0.438 | 0.437 | 0.437 | 0.439 | 0.446 | 0.447 |
| June | 0.404 | 0.406 | 0.409 | 0.408 | 0.415 | 0.420 | 0.430 | 0.433 | 0.431 | 0.431 | 0.433 | 0.440 | 0.441 |
| July | 0.403 | 0.405 | 0.408 | 0.407 | 0.414 | 0.419 | 0.429 | 0.431 | 0.430 | 0.430 | 0.432 | 0.439 | 0.440 |
| Aug. | 0.389 | 0.391 | 0.393 | 0.393 | 0.400 | 0.404 | 0.415 | 0.417 | 0.415 | 0.415 | 0.418 | 0.425 | 0.425 |
| Sept. | 0.376 | 0.378 | 0.381 | 0.380 | 0.387 | 0.391 | 0.401 | 0.404 | 0.402 | 0.402 | 0.404 | 0.411 | 0.412 |
| Oct. | 0.365 | 0.368 | 0.370 | 0.369 | 0.376 | 0.381 | 0.391 | 0.393 | 0.391 | 0.391 | 0.394 | 0.401 | 0.401 |
| Nov. | 0.368 | 0.371 | 0.373 | 0.372 | 0.379 | 0.384 | 0.394 | 0.396 | 0.395 | 0.395 | 0.397 | 0.404 | 0.405 |
| Dec. | 0.370 | 0.372 | 0.374 | 0.373 | 0.380 | 0.385 | 0.395 | 0.397 | 0.396 | 0.396 | 0.398 | 0.405 | 0.406 |

| RI Month | 2002 Oct. | Nov. | Dec. | 2003 Jan. | Feb. | Mar. | April | May | June | July | Aug. | Sept. | Oct. |
|---|---|---|---|---|---|---|---|---|---|---|---|---|
| **1991** Jan. | 0.366 | 0.369 | 0.371 | 0.370 | 0.377 | 0.382 | 0.392 | 0.394 | 0.392 | 0.392 | 0.395 | 0.402 | 0.402 |
| Feb. | 0.359 | 0.361 | 0.364 | 0.363 | 0.370 | 0.374 | 0.384 | 0.387 | 0.385 | 0.385 | 0.387 | 0.394 | 0.395 |
| March | 0.354 | 0.356 | 0.358 | 0.358 | 0.365 | 0.369 | 0.379 | 0.381 | 0.380 | 0.380 | 0.382 | 0.389 | 0.390 |
| April | 0.337 | 0.339 | 0.341 | 0.340 | 0.347 | 0.352 | 0.361 | 0.364 | 0.362 | 0.362 | 0.364 | 0.371 | 0.372 |
| May | 0.333 | 0.335 | 0.337 | 0.336 | 0.343 | 0.348 | 0.357 | 0.360 | 0.358 | 0.358 | 0.360 | 0.367 | 0.368 |
| June | 0.327 | 0.329 | 0.331 | 0.330 | 0.337 | 0.342 | 0.351 | 0.353 | 0.352 | 0.352 | 0.354 | 0.361 | 0.362 |
| July | 0.330 | 0.332 | 0.334 | 0.333 | 0.340 | 0.345 | 0.354 | 0.357 | 0.355 | 0.355 | 0.357 | 0.364 | 0.365 |
| Aug. | 0.327 | 0.329 | 0.331 | 0.330 | 0.337 | 0.342 | 0.351 | 0.353 | 0.352 | 0.352 | 0.354 | 0.361 | 0.362 |
| Sept. | 0.322 | 0.324 | 0.326 | 0.325 | 0.332 | 0.337 | 0.346 | 0.348 | 0.347 | 0.347 | 0.349 | 0.356 | 0.357 |
| Oct. | 0.317 | 0.319 | 0.321 | 0.321 | 0.327 | 0.332 | 0.341 | 0.343 | 0.342 | 0.342 | 0.344 | 0.351 | 0.352 |
| Nov. | 0.312 | 0.314 | 0.316 | 0.316 | 0.322 | 0.327 | 0.336 | 0.338 | 0.337 | 0.337 | 0.339 | 0.346 | 0.347 |
| Dec. | 0.311 | 0.313 | 0.315 | 0.315 | 0.321 | 0.326 | 0.335 | 0.338 | 0.336 | 0.336 | 0.338 | 0.345 | 0.346 |
| **1992** Jan. | 0.312 | 0.314 | 0.316 | 0.316 | 0.322 | 0.327 | 0.336 | 0.338 | 0.337 | 0.337 | 0.339 | 0.346 | 0.347 |
| Feb. | 0.305 | 0.307 | 0.310 | 0.309 | 0.315 | 0.320 | 0.329 | 0.332 | 0.330 | 0.330 | 0.332 | 0.339 | 0.340 |
| March | 0.301 | 0.304 | 0.305 | 0.305 | 0.312 | 0.316 | 0.326 | 0.328 | 0.326 | 0.326 | 0.328 | 0.335 | 0.336 |
| April | 0.282 | 0.284 | 0.286 | 0.285 | 0.292 | 0.296 | 0.305 | 0.308 | 0.306 | 0.306 | 0.308 | 0.315 | 0.316 |
| May | 0.277 | 0.279 | 0.281 | 0.281 | 0.287 | 0.291 | 0.301 | 0.303 | 0.302 | 0.302 | 0.304 | 0.310 | 0.311 |
| June | 0.277 | 0.279 | 0.281 | 0.281 | 0.287 | 0.291 | 0.301 | 0.303 | 0.302 | 0.302 | 0.304 | 0.310 | 0.311 |
| July | 0.282 | 0.284 | 0.286 | 0.285 | 0.292 | 0.296 | 0.305 | 0.308 | 0.306 | 0.306 | 0.308 | 0.315 | 0.316 |
| Aug. | 0.281 | 0.283 | 0.285 | 0.284 | 0.291 | 0.295 | 0.305 | 0.307 | 0.305 | 0.305 | 0.307 | 0.314 | 0.315 |
| Sept. | 0.276 | 0.278 | 0.280 | 0.280 | 0.286 | 0.291 | 0.300 | 0.302 | 0.301 | 0.301 | 0.303 | 0.309 | 0.310 |
| Oct. | 0.272 | 0.274 | 0.276 | 0.275 | 0.282 | 0.286 | 0.295 | 0.297 | 0.296 | 0.296 | 0.298 | 0.305 | 0.305 |
| Nov. | 0.273 | 0.276 | 0.278 | 0.277 | 0.283 | 0.288 | 0.297 | 0.299 | 0.298 | 0.298 | 0.300 | 0.306 | 0.307 |
| Dec. | 0.278 | 0.280 | 0.282 | 0.282 | 0.288 | 0.292 | 0.302 | 0.304 | 0.302 | 0.302 | 0.305 | 0.311 | 0.312 |
| **1993** Jan. | 0.290 | 0.292 | 0.294 | 0.294 | 0.300 | 0.305 | 0.314 | 0.316 | 0.315 | 0.315 | 0.317 | 0.323 | 0.324 |
| Feb. | 0.282 | 0.284 | 0.286 | 0.285 | 0.292 | 0.296 | 0.305 | 0.308 | 0.306 | 0.306 | 0.308 | 0.315 | 0.316 |
| March | 0.277 | 0.279 | 0.281 | 0.281 | 0.287 | 0.291 | 0.301 | 0.303 | 0.302 | 0.302 | 0.304 | 0.310 | 0.311 |
| April | 0.265 | 0.267 | 0.270 | 0.269 | 0.275 | 0.280 | 0.289 | 0.291 | 0.289 | 0.289 | 0.292 | 0.298 | 0.299 |
| May | 0.261 | 0.263 | 0.265 | 0.264 | 0.271 | 0.275 | 0.284 | 0.286 | 0.285 | 0.285 | 0.287 | 0.293 | 0.294 |
| June | 0.262 | 0.264 | 0.266 | 0.265 | 0.272 | 0.276 | 0.285 | 0.287 | 0.286 | 0.286 | 0.288 | 0.294 | 0.295 |
| July | 0.264 | 0.267 | 0.269 | 0.268 | 0.274 | 0.279 | 0.288 | 0.290 | 0.289 | 0.289 | 0.291 | 0.297 | 0.298 |
| Aug. | 0.259 | 0.261 | 0.263 | 0.263 | 0.269 | 0.273 | 0.282 | 0.285 | 0.283 | 0.283 | 0.285 | 0.292 | 0.292 |
| Sept. | 0.254 | 0.256 | 0.258 | 0.257 | 0.264 | 0.268 | 0.277 | 0.279 | 0.278 | 0.278 | 0.280 | 0.286 | 0.287 |
| Oct. | 0.255 | 0.257 | 0.259 | 0.258 | 0.264 | 0.269 | 0.278 | 0.280 | 0.279 | 0.279 | 0.281 | 0.287 | 0.288 |
| Nov. | 0.256 | 0.258 | 0.261 | 0.260 | 0.266 | 0.370 | 0.280 | 0.282 | 0.280 | 0.280 | 0.282 | 0.289 | 0.290 |
| Dec. | 0.254 | 0.256 | 0.258 | 0.257 | 0.264 | 0.268 | 0.277 | 0.279 | 0.278 | 0.278 | 0.280 | 0.286 | 0.287 |

| RI Month | 2002 Oct. | Nov. | Dec. | 2003 Jan. | Feb. | Mar. | April | May | June | July | Aug. | Sept. | Oct. |
|---|---|---|---|---|---|---|---|---|---|---|---|---|---|
| **1994** Jan. | 0.259 | 0.261 | 0.263 | 0.263 | 0.269 | 0.273 | 0.282 | 0.285 | 0.283 | 0.283 | 0.285 | 0.292 | 0.292 |
| Feb. | 0.252 | 0.254 | 0.256 | 0.255 | 0.262 | 0.266 | 0.275 | 0.277 | 0.276 | 0.276 | 0.278 | 0.284 | 0.285 |
| March | 0.248 | 0.251 | 0.253 | 0.252 | 0.258 | 0.262 | 0.272 | 0.274 | 0.272 | 0.272 | 0.274 | 0.281 | 0.281 |
| April | 0.234 | 0.236 | 0.238 | 0.237 | 0.243 | 0.248 | 0.257 | 0.259 | 0.257 | 0.257 | 0.259 | 0.266 | 0.266 |
| May | 0.229 | 0.232 | 0.234 | 0.233 | 0.239 | 0.243 | 0.252 | 0.254 | 0.253 | 0.253 | 0.255 | 0.261 | 0.262 |
| June | 0.229 | 0.232 | 0.234 | 0.233 | 0.239 | 0.243 | 0.252 | 0.254 | 0.253 | 0.253 | 0.255 | 0.261 | 0.262 |
| July | 0.235 | 0.238 | 0.240 | 0.239 | 0.245 | 0.249 | 0.258 | 0.260 | 0.259 | 0.259 | 0.261 | 0.267 | 0.268 |
| Aug. | 0.229 | 0.232 | 0.234 | 0.233 | 0.239 | 0.243 | 0.252 | 0.254 | 0.253 | 0.253 | 0.255 | 0.261 | 0.262 |
| Sept. | 0.227 | 0.229 | 0.231 | 0.230 | 0.237 | 0.241 | 0.250 | 0.252 | 0.250 | 0.250 | 0.252 | 0.259 | 0.259 |
| Oct. | 0.225 | 0.227 | 0.229 | 0.229 | 0.235 | 0.239 | 0.248 | 0.250 | 0.249 | 0.250 | 0.251 | 0.257 | 0.258 |
| Nov. | 0.224 | 0.226 | 0.228 | 0.228 | 0.234 | 0.238 | 0.247 | 0.249 | 0.248 | 0.248 | 0.250 | 0.256 | 0.257 |
| Dec. | 0.218 | 0.221 | 0.223 | 0.222 | 0.228 | 0.232 | 0.241 | 0.243 | 0.242 | 0.242 | 0.244 | 0.250 | 0.251 |
| **1995** Jan. | 0.218 | 0.221 | 0.223 | 0.222 | 0.228 | 0.232 | 0.241 | 0.243 | 0.242 | 0.242 | 0.244 | 0.250 | 0.251 |
| Feb. | 0.211 | 0.213 | 0.215 | 0.214 | 0.221 | 0.225 | 0.233 | 0.236 | 0.234 | 0.234 | 0.236 | 0.242 | 0.243 |
| March | 0.206 | 0.208 | 0.210 | 0.209 | 0.216 | 0.220 | 0.228 | 0.231 | 0.229 | 0.229 | 0.231 | 0.237 | 0.238 |
| April | 0.194 | 0.196 | 0.198 | 0.197 | 0.203 | 0.207 | 0.216 | 0.218 | 0.217 | 0.217 | 0.219 | 0.225 | 0.226 |
| May | 0.189 | 0.191 | 0.193 | 0.193 | 0.199 | 0.203 | 0.211 | 0.213 | 0.212 | 0.212 | 0.214 | 0.220 | 0.221 |
| June | 0.188 | 0.190 | 0.192 | 0.191 | 0.197 | 0.201 | 0.210 | 0.212 | 0.210 | 0.210 | 0.212 | 0.218 | 0.219 |
| July | 0.193 | 0.195 | 0.197 | 0.197 | 0.203 | 0.207 | 0.215 | 0.217 | 0.216 | 0.216 | 0.218 | 0.224 | 0.225 |
| Aug. | 0.187 | 0.189 | 0.191 | 0.190 | 0.196 | 0.200 | 0.209 | 0.211 | 0.209 | 0.209 | 0.211 | 0.217 | 0.218 |
| Sept. | 0.181 | 0.183 | 0.185 | 0.185 | 0.191 | 0.195 | 0.203 | 0.205 | 0.204 | 0.204 | 0.206 | 0.212 | 0.212 |
| Oct. | 0.188 | 0.190 | 0.192 | 0.191 | 0.197 | 0.201 | 0.210 | 0.212 | 0.210 | 0.210 | 0.212 | 0.218 | 0.219 |
| Nov. | 0.188 | 0.190 | 0.192 | 0.191 | 0.197 | 0.201 | 0.210 | 0.212 | 0.210 | 0.210 | 0.212 | 0.218 | 0.219 |
| Dec. | 0.180 | 0.182 | 0.184 | 0.184 | 0.190 | 0.194 | 0.202 | 0.204 | 0.203 | 0.203 | 0.205 | 0.211 | 0.212 |
| **1996** Jan. | 0.184 | 0.186 | 0.188 | 0.188 | 0.194 | 0.198 | 0.206 | 0.208 | 0.207 | 0.207 | 0.209 | 0.215 | 0.216 |
| Feb. | 0.179 | 0.181 | 0.183 | 0.182 | 0.188 | 0.192 | 0.201 | 0.203 | 0.201 | 0.201 | 0.203 | 0.209 | 0.210 |
| March | 0.174 | 0.176 | 0.178 | 0.178 | 0.183 | 0.187 | 0.196 | 0.198 | 0.197 | 0.197 | 0.199 | 0.205 | 0.205 |
| April | 0.166 | 0.168 | 0.170 | 0.169 | 0.175 | 0.179 | 0.187 | 0.189 | 0.188 | 0.188 | 0.190 | 0.196 | 0.197 |
| May | 0.164 | 0.165 | 0.167 | 0.167 | 0.173 | 0.177 | 0.185 | 0.187 | 0.186 | 0.186 | 0.188 | 0.194 | 0.194 |
| June | 0.163 | 0.165 | 0.167 | 0.166 | 0.172 | 0.176 | 0.184 | 0.186 | 01.85 | 0.185 | 0.187 | 0.193 | 0.193 |
| July | 0.167 | 0.169 | 0.171 | 0.171 | 0.177 | 0.180 | 0.189 | 0.191 | 0.190 | 0.190 | 0.192 | 0.198 | 0.198 |
| Aug. | 0.162 | 0.164 | 0.166 | 0.165 | 0.171 | 0.175 | 0.184 | 0.185 | 0.184 | 0.184 | 0.186 | 0.192 | 0.193 |
| Sept. | 0.157 | 0.159 | 0.161 | 0.160 | 0.166 | 0.170 | 0.178 | 0.180 | 0.179 | 0.179 | 0.181 | 0.187 | 0.187 |
| Oct. | 0.157 | 0.159 | 0.161 | 0.160 | 0.166 | 0.170 | 0.178 | 0.180 | 0.179 | 0.179 | 0.181 | 0.187 | 0.187 |
| Nov. | 0.156 | 0.158 | 0.160 | 0.159 | 0.165 | 0.169 | 0.177 | 0.179 | 0.178 | 0.178 | 0.180 | 0.186 | 0.186 |
| Dec. | 0.152 | 0.154 | 0.156 | 0.155 | 0.161 | 0.165 | 0.174 | 0.176 | 0.174 | 0.174 | 0.176 | 0.182 | 0.183 |

| RI Month | 2003 Oct. | Nov. | Dec. | 2003 Jan. | Feb. | Mar. | April | May | June | July | Aug. | Sept. | Oct. |
|---|---|---|---|---|---|---|---|---|---|---|---|---|---|
| **1997** Jan. | 0.152 | 0.154 | 0.156 | 0.155 | 0.161 | 0.165 | 0.174 | 0.176 | 0.174 | 0.174 | 0.176 | 0.182 | 0.183 |
| Feb. | 0.148 | 0.150 | 0.152 | 0.151 | 0.157 | 0.161 | 0.169 | 0.171 | 0.170 | 0.170 | 0.172 | 0.177 | 0.178 |
| March | 0.145 | 0.147 | 0.149 | 0.148 | 0.154 | 0.158 | 0.166 | 0.168 | 0.167 | 0.167 | 0.169 | 0.174 | 0.175 |
| April | 0.138 | 0.140 | 0.142 | 0.141 | 0.147 | 0.151 | 0.159 | 0.161 | 0.160 | 0.160 | 0.162 | 0.168 | 0.168 |
| May | 0.134 | 0.136 | 0.138 | 0.137 | 0.143 | 0.147 | 0.155 | 0.157 | 0.156 | 0.156 | 0.157 | 0.163 | 0.164 |
| June | 0.130 | 0.131 | 0.133 | 0.133 | 0.138 | 0.142 | 0.150 | 0.152 | 0.151 | 0.151 | 0.153 | 0.159 | 0.159 |
| July | 0.130 | 0.131 | 0.133 | 0.133 | 0.138 | 0.142 | 0.150 | 0.152 | 0.151 | 0.151 | 0.153 | 0.159 | 0.159 |
| Aug. | 0.122 | 0.124 | 0.126 | 0.126 | 0.131 | 0.135 | 0.143 | 0.145 | 0.144 | 0.144 | 0.146 | 0.151 | 0.152 |
| Sept. | 0.117 | 0.119 | 0.121 | 0.120 | 0.126 | 0.129 | 0.137 | 0.139 | 0.138 | 0.138 | 0.140 | 0.146 | 0.146 |
| Oct. | 0.115 | 0.117 | 0.119 | 0.118 | 0.124 | 0.128 | 0.136 | 0.138 | 0.137 | 0.137 | 0.139 | 0.144 | 0.145 |
| Nov. | 0.115 | 0.117 | 0.118 | 0.118 | 0.123 | 0.127 | 0.135 | 0.137 | 0.136 | 0.136 | 0.138 | 0.143 | 0.144 |
| Dec. | 0.112 | 0.114 | 0.116 | 0.115 | 0.121 | 0.124 | 0.133 | 0.134 | 0.133 | 0.133 | 0.135 | 0.141 | 0.141 |
| **1998** Jan. | 0.115 | 0.117 | 0.119 | 0.118 | 0.124 | 0.128 | 0.136 | 0.138 | 0.137 | 0.137 | 0.139 | 0.144 | 0.145 |
| Feb. | 0.110 | 0.112 | 0.114 | 0.113 | 0.119 | 0.122 | 0.130 | 0.132 | 0.131 | 0.131 | 0.133 | 0.138 | 0.139 |
| March | 0.106 | 0.108 | 0.110 | 0.109 | 0.115 | 0.119 | 0.127 | 0.129 | 0.127 | 0.127 | 0.129 | 0.135 | 0.136 |
| April | 0.094 | 0.096 | 0.098 | 0.097 | 0.103 | 0.106 | 0.114 | 0.116 | 0.115 | 0.115 | 0.117 | 0.122 | 0.123 |
| May | 0.088 | 0.090 | 0.092 | 0.091 | 0.097 | 0.100 | 0.108 | 0.110 | 0.109 | 0.109 | 0.111 | 0.116 | 0.117 |
| June | 0.089 | 0.091 | 0.092 | 0.092 | 0.097 | 0.101 | 0.109 | 0.111 | 0.110 | 0.110 | 0.111 | 0.117 | 0.118 |
| July | 0.091 | 0.093 | 0.095 | 0.094 | 0.100 | 0.104 | 0.112 | 0.113 | 0.112 | 0.112 | 0.114 | 0.120 | 0.120 |
| Aug. | 0.087 | 0.089 | 0.090 | 0.090 | 0.095 | 0.099 | 0.107 | 0.109 | 0.108 | 0.108 | 0.109 | 0.115 | 0.115 |
| Sept. | 0.082 | 0.084 | 0.086 | 0.085 | 0.091 | 0.094 | 0.102 | 0.104 | 0.103 | 0.103 | 0.105 | 0.110 | 0.111 |
| Oct. | 0.081 | 0.083 | 0.085 | 0.084 | 0.090 | 0.094 | 0.102 | 0.103 | 0.102 | 0.102 | 0.104 | 0.109 | 0.110 |
| Nov. | 0.082 | 0.084 | 0.086 | 0.085 | 0.091 | 0.094 | 0.102 | 0.104 | 0.103 | 0.103 | 0.105 | 0.110 | 0.111 |
| Dec. | 0.082 | 0.084 | 0.086 | 0.085 | 0.091 | 0.094 | 0.102 | 0.104 | 0.103 | 0.103 | 0.105 | 0.110 | 0.111 |
| **1999** Jan. | 0.089 | 0.091 | 0.092 | 0.092 | 0.097 | 0.101 | 0.109 | 0.111 | 0.110 | 0.110 | 0.111 | 0.117 | 0.118 |
| Feb. | 0.087 | 0.089 | 0.090 | 0.090 | 0.095 | 0.099 | 0.107 | 0.109 | 0.108 | 0.108 | 0.109 | 0.115 | 0.115 |
| March | 0.084 | 0.086 | 0.088 | 0.087 | 0.093 | 0.096 | 0.104 | 0.106 | 0.105 | 0.105 | 0.107 | 0.112 | 0.113 |
| April | 0.077 | 0.079 | 0.081 | 0.080 | 0.085 | 0.089 | 0.097 | 0.099 | 0.097 | 0.097 | 0.099 | 0.105 | 0.105 |
| May | 0.074 | 0.076 | 0.078 | 0.077 | 0.083 | 0.086 | 0.094 | 0.096 | 0.095 | 0.095 | 0.097 | 0.102 | 0.103 |
| June | 0.074 | 0.076 | 0.078 | 0.077 | 0.083 | 0.086 | 0.094 | 0.096 | 0.095 | 0.095 | 0.097 | 0.102 | 0.103 |
| July | 0.078 | 0.079 | 0.081 | 0.081 | 0.086 | 0.090 | 0.098 | 0.099 | 0.098 | 0.098 | 0.100 | 0.105 | 0.106 |
| Aug. | 0.075 | 0.077 | 0.079 | 0.078 | 0.083 | 0.087 | 0.095 | 0.097 | 0.095 | 0.095 | 0.097 | 0.103 | 0.103 |
| Sept. | 0.070 | 0.072 | 0.074 | 0.073 | 0.079 | 0.082 | 0.090 | 0.092 | 0.091 | 0.091 | 0.093 | 0.098 | 0.099 |
| Oct. | 0.068 | 0.070 | 0.072 | 0.071 | 0.077 | 0.080 | 0.088 | 0.090 | 0.089 | 0.089 | 0.091 | 0.096 | 0.097 |
| Nov. | 0.067 | 0.069 | 0.071 | 0.070 | 0.076 | 0.079 | 0.087 | 0.089 | 0.088 | 0.088 | 0.089 | 0.095 | 0.095 |
| Dec. | 0.063 | 0.065 | 0.067 | 0.066 | 0.072 | 0.075 | 0.083 | 0.085 | 0.084 | 0.084 | 0.085 | 0.091 | 0.091 |

| RI Month | 2002 Oct. | Nov. | Dec. | 2003 Jan. | Feb. | Mar. | April | May | June | July | Aug. | Sept. | Oct. |
|---|---|---|---|---|---|---|---|---|---|---|---|---|---|
| **2000** Jan. | 0.068 | 0.070 | 0.071 | 0.071 | 0.076 | 0.080 | 0.088 | 0.089 | 0.088 | 0.088 | 0.090 | 0.095 | 0.096 |
| Feb. | 0.062 | 0.064 | 0.066 | 0.065 | 0.070 | 0.074 | 0.082 | 0.084 | 0.082 | 0.082 | 0.084 | 0.090 | 0.090 |
| March | 0.056 | 0.058 | 0.060 | 0.059 | 0.065 | 0.068 | 0.076 | 0.078 | 0.077 | 0.077 | 0.078 | 0.084 | 0.084 |
| April | 0.046 | 0.048 | 0.049 | 0.049 | 0.054 | 0.058 | 0.065 | 0.067 | 0.066 | 0.066 | 0.068 | 0.073 | 0.073 |
| May | 0.042 | 0.044 | 0.046 | 0.045 | 0.050 | 0.054 | 0.062 | 0.063 | 0.062 | 0.062 | 0.064 | 0.069 | 0.070 |
| June | 0.040 | 0.041 | 0.043 | 0.043 | 0.048 | 0.051 | 0.059 | 0.061 | 0.060 | 0.060 | 0.061 | 0.067 | 0.067 |
| July | 0.043 | 0.045 | 0.047 | 0.046 | 0.052 | 0.055 | 0.063 | 0.065 | 0.063 | 0.063 | 0.065 | 0.070 | 0.071 |
| Aug. | 0.043 | 0.045 | 0.047 | 0.046 | 0.052 | 0.055 | 0.063 | 0.065 | 0.063 | 0.063 | 0.065 | 0.070 | 0.071 |
| Sept. | 0.036 | 0.038 | 0.040 | 0.039 | 0.044 | 0.048 | 0.055 | 0.057 | 0.056 | 0.056 | 0.058 | 0.063 | 0.063 |
| Oct. | 0.037 | 0.038 | 0.040 | 0.040 | 0.045 | 0.048 | 0.056 | 0.058 | 0.057 | 0.057 | 0.058 | 0.064 | 0.064 |
| Nov. | 0.034 | 0.035 | 0.037 | 0.037 | 0.042 | 0.045 | 0.053 | 0.055 | 0.053 | 0.053 | 0.055 | 0.060 | 0.061 |
| Dec. | 0.033 | 0.035 | 0.037 | 0.036 | 0.041 | 0.045 | 0.052 | 0.054 | 0.053 | 0.053 | 0.055 | 0.060 | 0.060 |
| **2001** Jan. | 0.040 | 0.041 | 0.043 | 0.043 | 0.048 | 0.051 | 0.059 | 0.061 | 0.060 | 0.060 | 0.061 | 0.067 | 0.067 |
| Feb. | 0.034 | 0.036 | 0.038 | 0.037 | 0.042 | 0.046 | 0.053 | 0.055 | 0.054 | 0.054 | 0.056 | 0.061 | 0.062 |
| March | 0.033 | 0.035 | 0.037 | 0.036 | 0.041 | 0.045 | 0.052 | 0.054 | 0.053 | 0.053 | 0.055 | 0.060 | 0.060 |
| April | 0.028 | 0.029 | 0.031 | 0.031 | 0.036 | 0.039 | 0.047 | 0.049 | 0.047 | 0.047 | 0.049 | 0.054 | 0.055 |
| May | 0.021 | 0.023 | 0.025 | 0.024 | 0.029 | 0.033 | 0.040 | 0.042 | 0.041 | 0.041 | 0.042 | 0.048 | 0.048 |
| June | 0.020 | 0.022 | 0.024 | 0.023 | 0.028 | 0.032 | 0.039 | 0.041 | 0.040 | 0.040 | 0.041 | 0.046 | 0.047 |
| July | 0.027 | 0.028 | 0.030 | 0.029 | 0.035 | 0.038 | 0.046 | 0.047 | 0.046 | 0.046 | 0.048 | 0.053 | 0.054 |
| Aug. | 0.022 | 0.024 | 0.026 | 0.025 | 0.030 | 0.034 | 0.041 | 0.043 | 0.042 | 0.042 | 0.044 | 0.049 | 0.049 |
| Sept. | 0.019 | 0.021 | 0.022 | 0.022 | 0.027 | 0.030 | 0.038 | 0.040 | 0.038 | 0.038 | 0.040 | 0.045 | 0.046 |
| Oct. | 0.021 | 0.022 | 0.024 | 0.024 | 0.029 | 0.032 | 0.040 | 0.041 | 0.040 | 0.040 | 0.042 | 0.047 | 0.048 |
| Nov. | 0.025 | 0.026 | 0.028 | 0.028 | 0.033 | 0.036 | 0.044 | 0.046 | 0.044 | 0.044 | 0.046 | 0.051 | 0.052 |
| Dec. | 0.026 | 0.028 | 0.029 | 0.029 | 0.034 | 0.037 | 0.045 | 0.047 | 0.046 | 0.046 | 0.047 | 0.052 | 0.053 |

| RI Month | 2002 Oct. | Nov. | Dec. | 2003 Jan. | Feb. | Mar. | April | May | June | July | Aug. | Sept. | Oct. |
|---|---|---|---|---|---|---|---|---|---|---|---|---|---|
| **2002** Jan. | 0.027 | 0.028 | 0.030 | 0.029 | 0.035 | 0.038 | 0.046 | 0.047 | 0.046 | 0.046 | 0.048 | 0.053 | 0.054 |
| Feb. | 0.024 | 0.025 | 0.027 | 0.026 | 0.032 | 0.035 | 0.043 | 0.044 | 0.043 | 0.043 | 0.045 | 0.050 | 0.051 |
| March | 0.019 | 0.021 | 0.023 | 0.022 | 0.028 | 0.031 | 0.038 | 0.040 | 0.039 | 0.039 | 0.041 | 0.046 | 0.046 |
| April | 0.013 | 0.014 | 0.016 | 0.015 | 0.020 | 0.024 | 0.031 | 0.033 | 0.032 | 0.032 | 0.034 | 0.039 | 0.039 |
| May | 0.010 | 0.011 | 0.013 | 0.012 | 0.018 | 0.021 | 0.028 | 0.030 | 0.029 | 0.029 | 0.031 | 0.036 | 0.036 |
| June | 0.010 | 0.011 | 0.013 | 0.012 | 0.018 | 0.021 | 0.028 | 0.030 | 0.029 | 0.029 | 0.031 | 0.036 | 0.036 |
| July | 0.011 | 0.013 | 0.015 | 0.014 | 0.019 | 0.023 | 0.030 | 0.032 | 0.031 | 0.031 | 0.032 | 0.038 | 0.038 |
| Aug. | 0.009 | 0.010 | 0.012 | 0.011 | 0.016 | 0.020 | 0.027 | 0.029 | 0.028 | 0.028 | 0.029 | 0.035 | 0.035 |
| Sept. | 0.002 | 0.003 | 0.005 | 0.005 | 0.010 | 0.013 | 0.020 | 0.022 | 0.021 | 0.021 | 0.023 | 0.028 | 0.028 |
| Oct. | — | 0.002 | 0.003 | 0.003 | 0.008 | 0.011 | 0.019 | 0.020 | 0.019 | 0.019 | 0.021 | 0.026 | 0.026 |
| Nov. |  | — | 0.002 | 0.001 | 0.006 | 0.010 | 0.017 | 0.019 | 0.017 | 0.017 | 0.019 | 0.024 | 0.025 |
| Dec. |  |  | — | Nil | 0.004 | 0.008 | 0.015 | 0.017 | 0.016 | 0.016 | 0.017 | 0.022 | 0.023 |
| **2003** Jan. |  |  |  | — | 0.005 | 0.008 | 0.016 | 0.017 | 0.016 | 0.016 | 0.018 | 0.023 | 0.024 |
| Feb. |  |  |  |  | — | 0.003 | 0.011 | 0.012 | 0.011 | 0.011 | 0.013 | 0.018 | 0.018 |
| Mar. |  |  |  |  |  | — | 0.007 | 0.009 | 0.008 | 0.008 | 0.009 | 0.014 | 0.015 |
| April |  |  |  |  |  |  | — | 0.002 | 0.001 | 0.001 | 0.002 | 0.007 | 0.008 |
| May |  |  |  |  |  |  |  | — | Nil | Nil | 0.001 | 0.006 | 0.006 |
| June |  |  |  |  |  |  |  |  | — | Nil | 0.002 | 0.007 | 0.007 |
| July |  |  |  |  |  |  |  |  |  | — | 0.002 | 0.007 | 0.007 |
| Aug. |  |  |  |  |  |  |  |  |  |  | — | 0.005 | 0.006 |
| Sept. |  |  |  |  |  |  |  |  |  |  |  | Nil | 0.001 |
| Oct. |  |  |  |  |  |  |  |  |  |  |  |  | Nil |

# Foreign exchange rates 2002–03

## Average rates for the year to 31 December 2002 and the year to 31 March 2003

| Country | Unit of currency | Average for year to 31 December 2002 | | Average for year to 31 March 2003 | |
|---|---|---|---|---|---|
| | | Currency units per £1 | Sterling value of currency unit (£) | Currency units per £1 | Sterling value of currency unit (£) |
| Algeria | Algerian Dinar | D.A. 119.1138 | 0.008395 | D.A. 122.9761 | 0.008132 |
| Argentina | Peso | $ 4.7816 | 0.20914 | $ 5.3381 | 0.18733 |
| Australia | Australian Dollar | $A. 2.8049 | 0.356519 | $A. 2.7925 | 0.358102 |
| Bahrain | Bahrain Dinar | B.D. 0.5671 | 1.763357 | B.D. 0.5836 | 1.713502 |
| Bangladesh | Taka | Tk. 86.7838 | 0.01152289 | Tk. 89.656 | 0.011154 |
| Barbados | Barbados Dollar | B.D.$ 3.0091 | 0.332325 | B.D.$ 3.0957 | 0.323029 |
| Bolivia | Boliviano | $.B. 10.8081 | 0.092523 | $.B. 11.3623 | 0.08801 |
| Botswana | Pula | P. 9.4098 | 0.10627218 | P. 9.1141 | 0.10972 |
| Brazil | Real | R$ 4.4345 | 0.2255 | R$ 4.9817 | 0.20073 |
| Brunei | Brunei Dollar | $ 2.691 | 0.37160907 | $ 2.7364 | 0.365444 |
| Burma | Burmese Kyat | K. 9.8609 | 0.10141 | K. 9.9464 | 0.10054 |
| Burundi | Burundi Franc | Fbu 1427.9542 | 0.0007003 | Fbu 1541.758 | 0.000649 |
| Canada | Canadian Dollar | Can. $ 2.3585 | 0.423998 | Can. $ 2.3955 | 0.417449 |
| Cayman Islands | C.I. Dollar | CI $ 1.2372 | 0.80827675 | CI $ 1.272 | 0.786164 |
| Chile | Chilean Peso | Ch. $ 1039.465 | 0.000962 | Ch. $ 1095.468 | 0.000913 |
| China | Renminb Yuan | RMBY 12.4779 | 0.08014169 | RMBY 12.8385 | 0.077891 |
| Columbia | Colombia Peso | Col. $ 3790.01 | 0.00026 | 4153.78 | 0.00024 |
| Congo Dem (Rep) (Zaire) | Congolese Franc | 525.7336 | 0.0019021 | 571.9449 | 0.0174842 |
| Costa Rica | Colon | C 544.9313 | 0.0018350995 | C 574.9884 | 0.001739 |
| Cuba | Cuban Peso | Po 31.6836 | 0.03156207 | Po 32.5763 | 0.030697 |
| Cyprus | Cyprus Pound | £C 0.9139 | 1.09421162 | £C 0.8945 | 1.117943 |
| Czech Republic | Koruna | KC 48.8242 | 0.02048165 | KC 47.7581 | 0.020939 |
| Denmark | Danish Krone | D. Kr. 11.8184 | 0.084614 | D. Kr. 11.5705 | 0.086427 |
| Ecuador | Sucre | S/.1.5077 | 0.66326192 | S/1.5513 | 0.644621 |
| Egypt | Egyptian Pound | LE 6.9638 | 0.1435998 | LE 7.4503 | 0.1342228 |
| El Salvador | Colon | C 13.197 | 0.0757748 | C 13.5688 | 0.073698 |
| Ethiopia | Ethiopian Birr | Br. 12.6417 | 0.07910329 | Br. 12.9708 | 0.077096 |
| European Union | Euro | € 1.5906 | 0.628694 | € 1.5573 | 0.642137 |
| Fiji Islands | Fiji Dollar | F$ 3.2671 | 0.30608185 | F$ 3.2512 | 0.307579 |
| French Cty/Africa | CFA Franc | CFAF 1042.0842 | 0.00095962 | CFAF 1017.883 | 0.000982 |
| French Pacific Is. | CFP Franc | CFPF 189.3468 | 0.00528131 | CFPF 184.3393 | 0.005425 |
| Gambia | Dalasi | D 30.1816 | 0.03313277 | D 33.5087 | 0.029843 |
| Ghana | Ghanaian Cedi | C. 12006.85 | 8.329 | C. 12669.67 | 7.893 |

## Average rates for the year to 31 December 2002 and the year to 31 March 2003

| Country | Unit of currency | Average for year to 31 December 2002 | | Average for year to 31 March 2003 | |
|---|---|---|---|---|---|
| | | Currency units per £1 | Sterling value of currency unit (£) | Currency units per £1 | Sterling value of currency unit (£) |
| Grenada & Windward Isles | East Caribbean Dollar | EC$. 4.0515 | 0.246822 | EC$. 4.1764 | 0.239441 |
| Guyana | Guyanese Dollar | G$ 270.7951 | 0.0036928 | G$ 278.0578 | 0.0035964 |
| Honduras | Lempira | L 24.7993 | 0.04032372 | L 25.8732 | 0.03865 |
| Hong Kong | H.K. Dollar | H.K.$ 11.7178 | 0.085340 | H.K.$ 12.4969 | 0.080020 |
| Hungary | Forint | Ft 385.0885 | 0.00259681 | Ft 376.5623 | 0.002656 |
| Iceland | Icelandic Krona | ISK 137.0658 | 0.007296 | ISK 132.2964 | 0.007559 |
| India | Indian Rupee | Re. 73.0477 | 0.01369 | Re. 74.8503 | 0.01336 |
| Indonesia | Indonesian Rupiah | Rp. 13992.992 | 7.146 | Rp. 13916.933 | 7.185 |
| Iran | Iranian Rial | RLS 5888.04 | 0.00017 | RLS 8472.51 | 0.00012 |
| Iraq | Iraq Dinar | ID 0.4679 | 2.13721 | ID 0.4814 | 2.07727 |
| Israel | New Shekel | NIS 7.1293 | 0.1402662 | NIS 7.4159 | 0.1348454 |
| Jamaica | Jamaican Dollar | J$ 72.6379 | 0.013767 | J$ 76.6837 | 0.013041 |
| Japan | Japanese Yen | Y 187.8315 | 0.005324 | Y 188.3036 | 0.005311 |
| Jordan | Jordanian Dinar | JD 1.0651 | 0.938879 | JD 1.0964 | 0.9120759 |
| Kenya | Kenyan Shilling | K Sh. 118.4879 | 0.00844 | K Sh. 121.3613 | 0.00824 |
| Korea (South) | Won | W 1875.2217 | 0.00053327 | W 1884.351 | 0.000531 |
| Kuwait | Kuwaiti Dinar | KD 0.4569 | 2.1886 | KD 0.4672 | 2.14041 |
| Laos | New Kip | KN 11466.425 | 8.72111 | KN 11789.48 | 8.48214 |
| Lebanon | Lebanese Pound | LL 2274.688 | 0.00044 | LL 2339.06 | 0.000428 |
| Libya | Libyan Dinar | LD 1.8923 | 0.5285 | LD 1.9259 | 0.5192 |
| Malawi | Malawi Kwacha | NK 115.074 | 0.00869 | NK 125.355 | 0.00798 |
| Malaysia | Ringgit | M$ 5.7167 | 0.174926 | M$ 5.882 | 0.17001 |
| Malta | Maltese Pound | Lm. 0.6505 | 1.53728 | Lm. 0.6451 | 1.55015 |
| Mauritius | Mauritian Rupee | Mau. Re. 45.0819 | 0.022182 | Mau. Re. 45.412 | 0.022021 |
| Mexico | Mexican Peso | N$ 14.5782 | 0.0686 | N$ 15.6552 | 0.06388 |
| Morocco | Dirham | DH 16.5284 | 0.06050192 | DH 16.3463 | 0.061176 |
| Nepal | Nepalese Rupee | N.Re. 116.3692 | 0.00859334 | N.Re. 119.1846 | 0.00839 |
| N'nd Antilles | Antilles Guilder | Na.f. 2.6856 | 0.37235627 | Na.f. 2.7612 | 0.362161 |
| New Zealand | N.Z. Dollar | $NZ 3.2393 | 0.3087087 | $NZ 3.1306 | 0.3194276 |
| Nicaragua | Gold Cordoba | GC$ 21.5082 | 0.0464939 | GC$ 22.4138 | 0.044615 |
| Nigeria | Nigerian Naira | N. 184.0362 | 0.005434 | N. 194.3859 | 0.005144 |
| Norway | Norwegian Krone | N. Kr. 11.954 | 0.083654 | N. Kr. 11.6072 | 0.086153 |
| Oman, Sultanate of | Rial Omani | RO 0.5792 | 1.726519 | RO 0.596 | 1.677852 |
| Pakistan | Pakistani Rupee | P.Re. 89.5939 | 0.011161 | P.Re. 91.3941 | 0.010942 |
| Papua New Guinea | Kina | K 5.9099 | 0.1692076 | K 6.095 | 0.164069 |
| Paraguay | Guarani | G 8691.2127 | 0.0001151 | G 9756.686 | 0.0001025 |

## Average rates for the year to 31 December 2002 and the year to 31 March 2003

| Country | Unit of currency | Average for year to 31 December 2002 | | Average for year to 31 March 2003 | |
|---|---|---|---|---|---|
| | | Currency units per £1 | Sterling value of currency unit (£) | Currency units per £1 | Sterling value of currency unit (£) |
| Peru | New Sol | $ 5.2931 | 0.18893 | $ 5.4531 | 0.18338 |
| Philippines | Philippine Peso | P 77.7051 | 0.01287 | P 81.0754 | 0.01233 |
| Poland | Zloty | Zl 6.1332 | 0.16307361 | Zl 6.2282 | 0.16056 |
| Qatar | Qatar Riyal | QR 5.4756 | 0.18263 | QR 5.6355 | 0.17745 |
| Romania | Leu | L 49889.0667 | 2.00445 | L 51638.82 | 1.98365 |
| Russia | Rouble (market rate) | R 47.4183 | 0.0210889 | R 49.0329 | 0.020394 |
| Rwanda | Rwanda Franc | RF 708.029 | 0.00141237 | RF 748.4881 | 0.001336 |
| Saudi Arabia | Saudi Riyal | S.Rls 5.641 | 0.17727 | S.Rls 5.805 | 0.17227 |
| Seychelles | Seychelles Rupee | SR 8.4761 | 0.11797879 | SR 8.7149 | 0.114746 |
| Sierra Leone | Leone | Le. 3094.516 | 0.000323 | Le. 3173.768 | 0.000315 |
| Singapore | Singapore Dollar | S$ 2.6899 | 0.37176 | S$ 2.7354 | 0.36558 |
| Solomon Islands | Sol. Islands Dollar | SI$ 10.4913 | 0.09531707 | SI$ 11.3636 | 0.088 |
| Somali Republic | Somali Shilling | SO. SH 3952.9042 | 0.00025298 | SO. SH 4064.276 | 0.000246 |
| South Africa | Rand | R 15.7465 | 0.063506 | R 14.9793 | 0.066759 |
| Sri Lanka | Sri Lanka Rupee | SLRe. 143.9681 | 0.006946 | SLRe. 149.2486 | 0.0067 |
| Sudan | Sudanese Dinar | LSd. 390.3116 | 0.00256206 | LSd. 401.9422 | 0.002488 |
| Surinam | Surinam Guilder | Sf. 3289.7917 | 0.00030425 | Sf. 3467.533 | 0.000288 |
| Swaziland | Lilangeli | L 15.5637 | 0.06425207 | L 14.788 | 0.067622 |
| Sweden | Swedish Krona | S.Kr. 14.5697 | 0.068636 | S.Kr. 14.2735 | 0.070060 |
| Switzerland | Swiss Franc | SwF 2.3336 | 0.428522 | SwF 2.2819 | 0.438231 |
| Syria | Syrian Pound | LS 74.7231 | 0.01338274 | LS 75.5653 | 0.013234 |
| Taiwan | New Taiwan Dollar | NT$ 51.97577 | 0.01924 | NT$ 53.3776 | 0.018734 |
| Tanzania | Tanzanian Shilling | T.Sh. 1452.96 | 0.00069 | T.Sh. 1522.58 | 0.00066 |
| Thailand | Thai Baht | B 64.6788 | 0.01546 | B 66.2242 | 0.0151 |
| Tonga Islands | Pa Anga | T$ 2.7637 | 0.36183377 | T$ 2.7496 | 0.363689 |
| Trinidad & Tobago | Trinidad & Tobago Dollar | TT$ 9.1895 | 0.10882 | TT$ 9.4752 | 0.105539 |
| Tunisia | Tunisian Dollar | D. 2.1331 | 0.4688 | D. 2.1332 | 0.46878 |
| Turkey | Turkish Lira | LT 2287542.21 | 4.3715 | LT 2464005.116 | 4.05843 |
| Uganda | New Shilling | U.Sh. 2704.318 | 0.00037 | U.Sh. 2840.852 | 0.000352 |
| United Arab Emirates | U.A.E. Dirham | Dh. 5.5247 | 0.1810053 | Dh. 5.6854 | 0.1758891 |
| Uruguay | Uruguayan Peso | $ 32.3184 | 0.03094 | $ 38.3931 | 0.02605 |
| USA | US Dollar | US$ 1.5023 | 0.665646 | US$ 1.5466 | 0.646580 |
| Venezuela | Ven. Bolivar | Bs. 1758.525 | 0.000569 | Bs. 2108.819 | 0.000474 |
| Vietnam | Dong | VND 23038.5083 | 0.000043 | VND 23813.17 | 0.000042 |
| Yemen | Yemen Rial | YRL 262.9526 | 0.00380297 | YRL 272.0802 | 0.003675 |

## Average rates for the year to 31 December 2002 and the year to 31 March 2003

| Country | Unit of currency | Average for year to 31 December 2002 | | Average for year to 31 March 2003 | |
|---|---|---|---|---|---|
| | | Currency units per £1 | Sterling value of currency unit (£) | Currency units per £1 | Sterling value of currency unit (£) |
| Zambia | Zambian Kwacha | K 6729.64 | 0.00015 | K 7137.79 | 0.00014 |
| Zimbabwe | Zimbabwe Dollar | Z$ 83.4043 | 0.01199 | Z$ 187.0132 | 0.005347 |

# Spot rates on 31 December 2002 and 31 March 2003

| Country | Unit of currency | 31 December 2002 | | 31 March 2003 | |
|---|---|---|---|---|---|
| | | Currency units per £1 | Sterling value of currency unit (£) | Currency units per £1 | Sterling value of currency unit (£) |
| Australia | Australian Dollar | $A. 2.859 | 0.3497726 | $A. 2.6157 | 0.3823068 |
| Canada | Canadian Dollar | Can.$ 2.5433 | 0.3931899 | Can.$ 2.3251 | 0.430089 |
| Denmark | Danish Krone | D. Kr. 11.3954 | 0.0877547 | D. Kr. 10.7573 | 0.0929601 |
| European Union | Euro | € 1.5342 | 0.6518055 | € 1.4486 | 0.6903216 |
| Hong Kong | Hong Kong Dollar | H.K.$ 12.5546 | 0.079652 | H.K.$ 12.3282 | 0.0811148 |
| Japan | Japanese Yen | Y 191.047 | 0.0052343 | Y 187.433 | 0.0053352 |
| Norway | Norwegian Krone | N. Kr. 11.153 | 0.0896619 | N. Kr. 11.4703 | 0.0971816 |
| South Africa | Rand | R 13.8138 | 0.0723913 | R 12.4413 | 0.0803774 |
| Sweden | Swedish Krone | S.Kr. 14.0276 | 0.071288 | S.Kr. 13.4023 | 0.074614 |
| Switzerland | Swiss Franc | SwF 2.226 | 0.4492362 | Sw.F. 2.1362 | 0.4681209 |
| USA | US Dollar | US$ 1.6099 | 0.6211565 | US$ 1.5807 | 0.6326311 |

# Double tax treaties

The UK has concluded a large number of tax treaties with other countries to avoid international double taxation and to prevent fiscal evasion. Tax treaties covering all usual areas of possible double taxation (comprehensive agreements) have been made, and those currently in force are indicated below by the letter 'C' in brackets. The table also notes agreements relating to shipping and air transport profits (S/A); air transport profits only (A); estates, inheritance and gifts (E/I/G); and social security contributions (SS).

| | | |
|---|---|---|
| Algeria (A) | Grenada (C) | Nigeria (C) |
| Antigua and Barbuda (C) | Guernsey (includes Alderney, | Norway (C/SS) |
| Argentina (C) | Herm and LIthou) (C/SS) | Oman (C) |
| Armenia[1] | Guyana (C) | Pakistan (C/E) |
| Australia (C/SS) | Hong Kong SAR (S/A) | Papua New Guinea (C) |
| Austria (C/SS) | Hungary (C) | Philippines (C/SS) |
| Azerbaijan (C)[1] | Iceland (C/SS) | Poland (C) |
| Bangladesh (C) | India (C/E) | Portugal (C/SS) |
| Barbados (C/SS) | Indonesia (C) | Romania (C) |
| Belarus (A)[1][3] | Iran (A) | Russian Federation (C)[1] |
| Belgium (C/SS) | Irish Republic (C/E/I/G/SS) | St. Christopher (St. Kitts) & Nevis (C) |
| Belize (C) | Isle of Man (C/SS) | Saudi Arabia (A) |
| Bermuda (SS) | Israel (C/SS) | Sierra Leone (C) |
| Bolivia (C) | Italy (C/E/SS) | Singapore (C) |
| Bosnia-Herzegovina (SS) | Ivory Coast (Cote d'Ivoire) (C) | Slovak Republic (C) |
| Botswana (C) | Jamaica (C/SS) | Slovenia (C/SS)[2] |
| Brazil (S/A) | Japan (C/SS) | Solomon Islands (C) |
| Brunei (C) | Jersey (C/SS) | South Africa (C/E/I/G) |
| Bulgaria (C) | Jordan (C) | Spain (C/SS) |
| Burma (Myanmar) (C) | Kazakstan (C)[1] | Sri Lanka (C) |
| Cameroon (A) | Kenya (C) | Sudan (C) |
| Canada (C/SS) | Kiribati & Tuvalu (C) | Swaziland (C) |
| Chile (C)[3] | Korean Republic (C/SS) | Sweden (C/E/I/G/SS) |
| China (C/A) | Kuwait (C) | Switzerland (C/E/SS) |
| Croatia (C/SS)[2] | Kyrgystan[1] | Taiwan (C) |
| Cyprus (C/SS) | Latvia (C)[1] | Tajikistan (C)[1] |
| Czech Republic (C) | Lebanon (S/A) | Thailand (C) |
| Denmark (C/SS) | Lesotho (C) | Trinidad and Tobago (C) |
| Egypt (C) | Lithuania (C)[1] | Tunisia (C) |
| Estonia (C)[1] | Luxembourg (C/SS) | Turkey (C/SS) |
| Ethiopia (A) | Macedonia (C/SS)[2] | Tuvalu (C) |
| Falkland Islands (C) | Malawi (C) | Turkmenistan (C)[1] |
| Fiji (C) | Malaysia (C) | Uganda (C) |
| Finland (C/SS) | Malta (C/SS) | Ukraine (C) |
| France (includes Guadeloupe, | Mauritius (C/SS) | USA (C/E/I/G/SS) |
| Guyane, Martinique and | Mexico (C) | Uzbekistan (C/A)[1] |
| Réunion (C/E/SS) | Moldova[1] | Venezuela (C) |
| Gambia (C) | Mongolia (C) | Vietnam (C) |
| Georgia[1] | Montserrat (C) | Yugoslavia (C/SS)[2] |
| Germany (C/SS) | Morocco (C) | Zaire (S/A) |
| Ghana (C) | Namibia (C) | Zambia (C) |
| Gibraltar (SS) | Netherlands (C/E/I/G/SS) | Zimbabwe (C) |
| Greece (C) | New Zealand (C/SS) | |

**Notes**

[1] See SP 4/01 for the status of the Convention of 31 July 1985 with the former USSR. For former Soviet republics, there are a variety of options as to whether or not a treaty is in force. See separate table below for the position as at April 2003.

[2] See SP 6/93 for the status of the Convention of 5 November 1981 with the former Yugoslavia.

[3] The following treaties were signed and agreed, but not in force, at the time of publication:

* Belarus (C) (see also footnote [1] above);

* Chile (C);

The reciprocal social security arrangements made with EU member states have all, with the exception of parts of the Orders relating to Germany, been superseded by EC Regulation 1408/71 (as codified and amended). See Leaflet SA 29 for social security rights in the EU.

# Double tax treaties – former territories of the USSR

There are four possible options for an independent country that was once part of the USSR:

- the former UK/USSR treaty could still apply;
- a new, separately negotiated, treaty might apply in place of any previous agreement;
- the former UK/USSR treaty might no longer apply, but no separate treaty be in place yet for the independent country; or
- a new, separate, treaty might be in process of negotiation.

The following table summarises the position detailed in SP 4/01.

| Country | UK/USSR treaty in force | Own treaty in force | UK/USSR treaty NOT Applicable (and no separate treaty) | Treaty Pending? (Neg = being negotiated; NYR = awaiting ratification) |
|---|---|---|---|---|
| Armenia | to April 2002[1] | NO | from April 2002 | NO |
| Azerbaijan | to April/January 1996 | from April/January 1996 | – | – |
| Belarus | YES – pending own treaty | See Pending | – | YES (NYR) |
| Estonia | to April/January 1995[2] | from April/January 1995 | – | – |
| Georgia | to April 2002[1] | See Pending | from April 2002 | Neg |
| Kazakhstan | to April/January 1993 | from April/January 1993 | – | – |
| Kyrgyzstan | to April 2002[1] | NO | from April 2002 | NO |
| Latvia | to April/January 1997[2] | from April/January 1997 | – | – |
| Lithuania | to April 2002[2] | from April/January 2002 | from April 2002[2] | – |
| Moldova | to April 2002[1] | NO | from April 2002 | NO |
| Russian Federation | to April/January 1998 | from April/January 1998 | – | – |
| Tajikistan | YES | NO | – | NO |
| Turkmenistan | YES | NO | – | NO |
| Ukraine | to April/January 1994[3] | from April/January 1994[3] | – | – |
| Uzbekistan | to April/January 1995 | from April/January 1995 | – | – |

**Notes**

[1] Armenia, Georgia, Kyrgyzstan and Moldova have indicated that they are no longer bound by the terms of the UK/USSR treaty.

[2] Estonia, Latvia and Lithuania have indicated that they consider themselves never to have been bound by the UK/USSR treaty. In practice, the UK has been operating as if the UK/USSR treaty has been in force for these periods, subject to the position of Lithuania per the table.

[3] The date the UK/Ukraine treaty comes into force is dependent in some instances on the nature of the income in the Ukraine.

# Clearance procedures

| Subject | Statutory reference etc. | Application submitted to: |
|---|---|---|
| Maintenance funds for historic buildings | IHTA 1984, Sch. 4, para. 1 | Inland Revenue Capital Taxes Office Ferrers House PO Box 38 Castle Meadow Road Nottingham NG2 1BB |
| Leases granted at an undervalue | ICTA 1988, s. 35 | Inspector of taxes |
| Demergers; purchase of own shares; transactions in securities; share exchanges reconstructions involving the transfer of a business; transfer of a trade between EU member states; transfer of a non-UK trade between EU member states; intangible fixed assets | ICTA 1988, s. 215, 225, 707; TCGA 1992, s. 138(1), 139(5), 140B, 140D; FA 2002, Sch. 29, para. 88 | Mohini Sawhney Fifth Floor 22 Kingsway London WC2B 6NR<br><br>But where the application is market sensitive, send to Ray McCann at the same address |
| Transfers of long-term business between life assurance companies | ICTA 1988, s. 444A, TCGA 1992, s. 211 | Robert Peel Revenue Policy, Business Tax Room 5W2, 5th Floor 22 Kingsway London WC2B 6NR<br><br>But where at least one party is a non-UK resident company or a friendly society, applications to<br><br>Richard Thomas Revenue Policy, Business Tax Room 5W2, 5th Floor 22 Kingsway London WC2B 6NR |
| Employee share schemes; profit sharing schemes; savings related share option schemes; employee share option schemes | ICTA 1988, Sch. 9 | Kevin Meehan Revenue Policy, Capital and Savings Employee Share Schemes 2nd Floor, New Wing Somerset House London WC2 1LB |
| Occupational and personal pensions, public sector schemes, FSAVC schemes and ex gratia relevant payments | ICTA 1988, s. 590, 591 | Inland Revenue Pension Schemes Office Yorke House PO Box 62 Castle Meadow Road Nottingham NG2 1BG |
| Controlled foreign companies | ICTA 1988, s. 747–756, Sch. 24–26 | Stephen Hewitt Revenue Policy, International Business Tax Group (CFC Clearances) Victory House 30–34 Kingsway London WC2B 6ES |

| Subject | Statutory reference etc. | Application submitted to: |
|---|---|---|
| Transactions in shares or debentures; Notification of transactions falling within the European Capital Movements Directive | ICTA 1988, s. 765, 765A | Mark Ritchie<br>Revenue Policy, International Business Tax Group<br>(Treasury Consent)<br>Victory House<br>30–34 Kingsway<br>London WC2B 6ES |
| Transactions in land | ICTA 1988, s. 776 | Inspector of taxes |
| Certification of qualifying life assurance policies | ICTA 1988, Sch. 15 | Claire Ritchie<br>Revenue Policy, Business Tax<br>(Insurance)<br>Room 5W4, 5th Floor<br>22 Kingsway<br>London WC2B 6NR |
| Company migrations | FA 1988, s. 130 | Mark Ritchie<br>Revenue Policy, International Business Tax Group<br>(Company Migrations)<br>Victory House<br>30–34 Kingsway<br>London WC2B 6ES |
| Advance Pricing Agreements | FA 1999, s. 85–87 | Ian Wood<br>Revenue Policy, International Business Tax Group<br>(APAs)<br>Victory House<br>30–34 Kingsway<br>London WC2B 6ES<br><br>For APAs involving oil taxation:<br>Janice Cross<br>Revenue Policy, International Oil Taxation Office (APAs)<br>Melbourne House<br>Aldwych<br>London WC2 4LL |
| Corporate venturing schemes | FA 2000, Sch. 15, para. 89 | Small Company Enterprise Centre<br>TIDO<br>Ty Glas<br>Llanishen<br>Cardiff CF14 5ZG |

| Subject | Statutory reference etc. | Application submitted to: |
|---|---|---|
| Withholding tax on non-resident entertainers and sportsmen | SI 1987/530 | Foreign Entertainers Unit<br>Special Compliance Office<br>Birmingham<br>Royal House<br>Prince's Gate<br>2–6 Homer Road<br>Solihull<br>West Midlands<br>B91 3WG |
| Pre-transaction advice on funding issues | Tax Bulletin, issues 17 and 37 | Dave Smith<br>Revenue Policy, International Business Tax Group (Advice on funding)<br>Victory House<br>30–34 Kingsway<br>London WC2 6ES |

# Recognised stock exchanges

'The Stock Exchange' (strictly known as 'The International Stock Exchange of the United Kingdom and the Republic of Ireland Ltd') is a 'recognised stock exchange'; the stock exchanges of the following countries have also been designated by the Board of Inland Revenue as 'recognised stock exchanges'. Where there is no specific or unified exchange shown there is included any exchange recognised by the laws of that country (ICTA 1988, s. 841; TCGA 1992, s. 288(1)).

Note that the Revenue explained a revised interpretation of 'listed on a recognised stock exchange' in a press release of 28 November 2001. This had the effect of reversing the previous view of securities traded on EU 'junior' markets and NASDAQ Europe (formerly EASDAQ) which are now treated as unlisted (although with transitional provisions in place).

In a Policy Statement dated 27 November 2002 the Revenue announced that it would be taking a more broadly-based approach.

| | | |
|---|---|---|
| Australia (and subsidiaries) | Hong Kong | Portugal |
| Austria | Ireland[1] | Singapore (unified) |
| Belgium (inc. NASDAQ Europe) | Italy | South Africa (Johannesburg) |
| Brazil (Rio de Janeiro, São Paulo) | Japan | Spain |
| Canada | Korea | Sri Lanka (Colombo) |
| Denmark (Copenhagen) | Luxembourg | Sweden (Stockholm) |
| Finland (Helsinki) | Malaysia (Kuala Lumpur) | Switzerland |
| France | Mexico | Thailand |
| Germany | Netherlands | United States (inc. NASDAQ) |
| Greece (Athens) | New Zealand (unified) | |
| | Norway | |

**Note**

[1] Since 25 March 1973 the stock exchange in Ireland has been included within 'The Stock Exchange'.

# Recognised futures exchanges

The following futures exchanges have been designated by the Board of Inland Revenue as 'recognised futures exchanges' (TCGA 1992, s. 288(6))[1]:

| Date | Exchange |
|---|---|
| From 6 August 1985 | International Petroleum Exchange of London<br>London Metal Exchange<br>London Wool Terminal Market |
| From 12 December 1985 | London Gold Market<br>London Silver Market |
| From 19 December 1986 | Chicago Mercantile Exchange<br>Philadelphia Board of Trade<br>New York Mercantile Exchange |
| From 24 April 1987 | Chicago Board of Trade |
| From 29 July 1987 | Montreal Exchange<br>Mid-America Commodity Exchange |
| From 15 December 1987 | Hong Kong Futures Exchange<br>New York Coffee Sugar and Cocoa Exchange |
| From 25 August 1988 | Commodity Exchange, Inc (COMEX)<br>Citrus Associates of the New York Cotton Exchange Inc<br>New York Cotton Exchange |
| From 31 October 1988 | Sydney Futures Exchange Ltd |
| From 18 March 1992 | OM Stockholm<br>London Commodity Exchange[2]<br>OMLX (formerly OM London) |
| From 22 March 1992 | London International Financial Futures and Options Exchange (LIFFE)[3] |

**Notes**

[1] When the Board recognises a futures exchange this is announced in the *London Gazette*.

[2] The following futures exchanges, which are recognised from 6 August 1985, are now part of the London Commodity Exchange: Baltic International Freight Futures Exchange; London Cocoa Terminal Market; London Coffee Terminal Market; London Futures and Options Exchange; London Grain Futures Market; London Meat Futures Market; London Potato Futures Market; London Rubber Market; London Soya Bean Meal Futures Market; London Sugar Terminal Market. The name of the London International Financial Futures Exchange changed to London Commodity Exchange from 1 July 1993.

[3] The London International Financial Futures Exchange and the London Traded Options Market merged on 22 March 1992, forming the London International Financial Futures and Options Exchange (LIFFE).

## Recognised clearing systems

The following clearing systems have been designated by the Board of Inland Revenue as 'recognised clearing systems' (ICTA 1988, s. 841A, for the purposes of s. 124(2)):

| Country | Clearing system | Effective date |
|---|---|---|
| Belgium | Euroclear | 26 July 1984 |
| Luxembourg | Cedel | 26 July 1984 |
| United Kingdom | Bank of England European Settlements Office | 16 August 1993 |
| | First Chicago Clearing Centre | 14 October 1988 |
| United States | The Depository Trust Co | 18 July 1995 |

**Note**

ICTA 1988, s. 841A is repealed for payments of interest made on or after 1 April 2001 (FA 2000, s. 156 and Sch. 40, Pt. II(17))

## Recognised investment exchanges

Regulations may designate 'recognised investment exchanges' within the meaning of the *Financial Services Act* 1986, s. 37(3) so that securities traded on such exchanges are treated in the same way for tax purposes as those traded on 'The Stock Exchange' (strictly known as 'The International Stock Exchange of the United Kingdom and the Republic of Ireland Ltd') (FA 1986, Sch. 18, para. 8; F(No. 2)A 1987, s. 73; ICTA 1988, s. 841(3)).

*From 22 March 1992*: London International Financial Futures Exchange (Administration and Management) (LIFFE (A & M)).

# TAXATION OF CAPITAL GAINS

## Reliefs, rates and thresholds

| Tax year | Annual exempt amount | | Chattel exemption (max sale proceeds)[1] | Rate | |
|---|---|---|---|---|---|
| | Individuals, PRs[2], trusts for mentally disabled[3] £ | Other trusts[3] £ | £ | Individuals % | Trustees and PRs % |
| 2004–05 | 8,200 | 4,100 | 6,000 | 10/20/40[4] | 34 |
| 2003–04 | 7,900 | 3,950 | 6,000 | 10/20/40[4] | 34 |
| 2002–03 | 7,700 | 3,850 | 6,000 | 10/20/40[4] | 34 |
| 2001–02 | 7,500 | 3,750 | 6,000 | 10/20/40[4] | 34 |
| 2000–01 | 7,200 | 3,600 | 6,000 | 10/20/40[4] | 34 |
| 1999–2000 | 7,100 | 3,550 | 6,000 | 20/40[4] | 34 |
| 1998–99 | 6,800 | 3,400 | 6,000 | 20/23/40[4] | 34[6] |
| 1997–98 | 6,500 | 3,250 | 6,000 | 20/23/40[4] | 23[5] |

**Notes**

[1] Where disposal proceeds exceed the exemption limit, marginal relief restricts any chargeable gain to $\frac{5}{3}$ of the excess. Where there is a loss and the proceeds are less than £6,000 the proceeds are deemed to be £6,000.

[2] For year of death and next two years in the case of personal representatives (PRs) of the deceased persons.

[3] Multiple trusts created by the same settlor; each attracts relief to the annual amount divided by the number of such trusts (subject to a minimum of 10% of the full amount).

[4] For 2000–01 onwards capital gains tax rates are 10% where gains added to total income are below the starting rate limit, 20% where they are below the basic rate limit, and 40% where they exceed the basic rate limit.

[5] The rate of tax applicable to trustees of discretionary trusts is a flat rate of 34% for 1996–97 onwards.

[6] For 1998–99 onwards, the flat rate of 34% applicable to trusts also applies to all gains realised by trustees and personal representatives of deceased persons.

## Taper relief

(TCGA 1992, s. 2A and Sch. A1)

(applies to individuals, trustees and personal representatives, NOT companies)

Introduced for gains realised on or after 6 April 1998.

The chargeable gain is reduced according to how long the asset has been held or treated as held after 5 April 1998. For disposals on or before 5 April 2000, all assets acquired prior to 17 March 1998 qualify for an addition of one year to the period for which they are treated as held after 5 April 1998. For disposals on or after 6 April 2000, only non-business assets qualify for the additional year.

The taper is generally applied to the net chargeable gain for the year after deduction of any losses of the same tax year and of any losses carried forward from earlier years.

The relief is more generous for business assets, defined as:

- an asset used for the purposes of a trade carried on by the individual;
- an asset held for the purposes of a qualifying office or employment; or
- qualifying shareholding in a 'qualifying' company.

On or before 5 April 2000, a 'qualifying' company is a trading company (or holding company of a trading group), and a qualifying shareholding is one in which the individual holds shares in a qualifying company which entitle that individual to exercise at least:

- 5 per cent of the voting rights and the individual is a full-time working officer or full-time employee of that company; or
- 25 per cent of the voting rights.

On or after 6 April 2000, the definition of a 'qualifying' company is extended to include a non-trading company (or holding company of a non-trading group). Generally, a qualifying shareholding comprises:

- all shareholdings in unlisted trading companies;
- shareholdings in a listed trading company where the individual is an employee or an officer, including those involved on a part-time basis;
- shareholdings in a listed trading company where the individual is able to exercise at least five per cent of the voting rights in the company; and
- shareholdings in a listed or unlisted non-trading company where the individual is an employee or an officer who does not have a material interest (generally, not more than a 10 per cent shareholding) in the company.

Where shares qualify as a business asset only from 6 April 2000, an apportionment of the eventual gain is necessary so that part qualifies for business taper and the balance for non-business taper.

### Non-business assets – gains of 1998–99 onwards

| Gains on non-business assets | | |
|---|---|---|
| Number of *complete* years after 5/4/98 for which asset held | Percentage of gain chargeable | Equivalent tax rates |
| 0 | 100 | 40/20/10 |
| 1 | 100 | 40/20/10 |
| 2 | 100 | 40/20/10 |
| 3 | 95 | 38/19/9.5 |
| 4 | 90 | 36/18/9 |
| 5 | 85 | 34/17/8.5 |
| 6 | 80 | 32/16/8 |
| 7 | 75 | 30/15/7.5 |
| 8 | 70 | 28/14/7 |
| 9 | 65 | 26/13/6.5 |
| 10 or more | 60 | 24/12/6 |

### Business assets – gains of 2002–03 onwards

| Gains on business assets | | |
|---|---|---|
| Number of *complete* years after 5/4/98 for which asset held | Percentage of gain chargeable | Equivalent tax rates |
| 0 | 100 | 40/20/10 |
| 1 | 50 | 20/10/5 |
| 2 or more | 25 | 10/5/2.5 |

**2000–01 and 2001–02**

| Gains on business assets | | |
|---|---|---|
| Number of *complete* years after 5/4/98 for which asset held | Percentage of gain chargeable | Equivalent tax rates |
| 0 | 100 | 40/20/10 |
| 1 | 87.5 | 35/17.5/8.75 |
| 2 | 75 | 30/15/7.5 |
| 3 | 50 | 20/10/5 |
| 4 or more | 25 | 10/5/2.5 |

**1998–99 and 1999–2000**

| Gains on business assets | |
|---|---|
| Number of *complete* years after 5/4/98 for which asset held | Percentage of gain chargeable |
| 0 | 100 |
| 1 | 92.5 |
| 2 | 85 |
| 3 | 77.5 |

# Roll-over relief

(TCGA 1992, s. 152)

To qualify for roll-over or hold-over relief on the replacement of business assets, the items must be appropriate business assets (see below) and the reinvestment must generally take place within 12 months before, or three years after, the disposal of the old asset. For hold-over relief, the replacement asset is a depreciating asset (an asset with a predictable useful life of no more than 60 years).

Classes of assets qualifying for relief:

- land and buildings occupied and used exclusively for the purposes of a trade;
- fixed plant or fixed machinery (which does not form part of a building);
- ships, aircraft, hovercraft;
- satellites, space stations and spacecraft (including launch vehicles);
- goodwill;
- milk quotas, potato quotas and fish quotas;
- ewe and suckler cow premium quotas; and
- Lloyd's member's syndicate rights and assets treated as acquired, under FA 1999, s. 73, by members.

## Retirement relief

(TCGA 1992, s. 163–164 and Sch. 6)

Retirement relief exempts from CGT a certain proportion of the gain from the disposal of a business by an individual who is aged 50 or over, or who retires earlier due to ill health.

It is phased out from 6 April 1999 by a gradual reduction of the relief thresholds and ceased to be available from 6 April 2003.

The annual thresholds are as follows:

| Year | 100% relief on gains up to: £ | 50% relief on gains between: £ |
|---|---|---|
| 2003–04 | none | none |
| 2002–03 | 50,000 | 50,001–200,000 |
| 2001–02 | 100,000 | 100,001–400,000 |
| 2000–01 | 150,000 | 150,001–600,000 |
| 1999–2000 | 200,000 | 200,001–800,000 |
| 1994–95 to 1998–99 | 250,000 | 250,001–1,000,000 |
| 1993–94 (to 28/11/93) | 150,000 | 150,000–600,000 |
| 1993–94 (from 29/11/93) | 250,000 | 250,000–1,000,000 |

## Due date for payment

(TCGA 1992, s. 7)

### 1996–97 and subsequent years

31 January following tax year in which gain accrued.

## Leases which are wasting assets

**Restrictions of allowable expenditure** (TCGA 1992, s. 240 and Sch. 8, para. 1)

Fraction equal to $\dfrac{P(1) - P(3)}{P(1)}$ excluded from base cost,

and fraction equal to $\dfrac{P(2) - P(3)}{P(2)}$ excluded from other expenditure where:

P(1) = table percentage for duration of lease at time of acquisition (or 31 March 1982 where applicable);

P(2) = table percentage for duration of lease at time expenditure incurred; and

P(3) = table percentage for duration of lease at time of disposal

| Years | % | Monthly[1] increment | Years | % | Monthly[1] increment | Years | % | Monthly[1] increment |
|---|---|---|---|---|---|---|---|---|
| 50 or more | 100 | — | 33 | 90.280 | .073 | 16 | 64.116 | .196 |
| 49 | 99.657 | .029 | 32 | 89.354 | .077 | 15 | 61.617 | .208 |
| 48 | 99.289 | .031 | 31 | 88.371 | .082 | 14 | 58.971 | .221 |
| 47 | 98.902 | .032 | 30 | 87.330 | .087 | 13 | 56.167 | .234 |
| 46 | 98.490 | .034 | 29 | 86.226 | .092 | 12 | 53.191 | .247 |
| 45 | 98.059 | .036 | 28 | 85.053 | .098 | 11 | 50.038 | .263 |
| 44 | 97.595 | .039 | 27 | 83.816 | .103 | 10 | 46.695 | .279 |
| 43 | 97.107 | .041 | 26 | 82.496 | .110 | 9 | 43.154 | .295 |
| 42 | 96.593 | .043 | 25 | 81.100 | .116 | 8 | 39.399 | .313 |
| 41 | 96.041 | .046 | 24 | 79.622 | .123 | 7 | 35.414 | .332 |
| 40 | 95.457 | .049 | 23 | 78.055 | .131 | 6 | 31.195 | .352 |
| 39 | 94.842 | .051 | 22 | 76.399 | .138 | 5 | 26.722 | .373 |
| 38 | 94.189 | .054 | 21 | 74.635 | .147 | 4 | 21.983 | .395 |
| 37 | 93.497 | .058 | 20 | 72.770 | .155 | 3 | 16.959 | .419 |
| 36 | 92.761 | .061 | 19 | 70.791 | .165 | 2 | 11.629 | .444 |
| 35 | 91.981 | .065 | 18 | 68.697 | .175 | 1 | 5.983 | .470 |
| 34 | 91.156 | .069 | 17 | 66.470 | .186 | 0 | 0 | .499 |

**Note**

[1] Where duration is *not* an *exact* number of years, the table percentage for the whole number of years is increased by $\frac{1}{12}$ of the difference between that and the next highest percentage for each odd month. Fourteen odd days or more are rounded up and treated as a month; less than 14 odd days are ignored.

# Premiums for short leases – CGT/IT charge

The chart below shows the proportion of any premium received in respect of a lease of less than 50 years which is chargeable to capital gains tax and that which is chargeable to income tax (ICTA 1988, s. 34).

| Length of lease in years | Amount chargeable to CGT % | Income tax Sch. A % |
|---|---|---|
| Over 50 | 100 | 0 |
| 50 | 98 | 2 |
| 49 | 96 | 4 |
| 48 | 94 | 6 |
| 47 | 92 | 8 |
| 46 | 90 | 10 |
| 45 | 88 | 12 |
| 44 | 86 | 14 |
| 43 | 84 | 16 |
| 42 | 82 | 18 |
| 41 | 80 | 20 |
| 40 | 78 | 22 |
| 39 | 76 | 24 |
| 38 | 74 | 26 |
| 37 | 72 | 28 |
| 36 | 70 | 30 |
| 35 | 68 | 32 |
| 34 | 66 | 34 |
| 33 | 64 | 36 |

| Length of lease in years | Amount chargeable to CGT % | Income tax Sch. A % |
|---|---|---|
| 32 | 62 | 38 |
| 31 | 60 | 40 |
| 30 | 58 | 42 |
| 29 | 56 | 44 |
| 28 | 54 | 46 |
| 27 | 52 | 48 |
| 26 | 50 | 50 |
| 25 | 48 | 52 |
| 24 | 46 | 54 |
| 23 | 44 | 56 |
| 22 | 42 | 58 |
| 21 | 40 | 60 |
| 20 | 38 | 62 |
| 19 | 36 | 64 |
| 18 | 34 | 66 |
| 17 | 32 | 68 |
| 16 | 30 | 70 |
| 15 | 28 | 72 |
| 14 | 26 | 74 |
| 13 | 24 | 76 |
| 12 | 22 | 78 |
| 11 | 20 | 80 |
| 10 | 18 | 82 |
| 9 | 16 | 84 |
| 8 | 14 | 86 |
| 7 | 12 | 88 |
| 6 | 10 | 90 |
| 5 | 8 | 92 |
| 4 | 6 | 94 |
| 3 | 4 | 96 |
| 2 | 2 | 98 |
| 1 or less | 0 | 100 |

# Indexation allowance

For disposals on or after 6 April 1998, individuals and trustees, within the charge to capital gains tax, are not entitled to indexation allowance in respect of any period after April 1998. Companies subject to corporation tax on their chargeable gains continue to be entitled to indexation allowance.

For tables showing the retail prices index figures and indexed rise concerning recent disposals, see p. 72.

**Capital gains tax: disposals after 5 April 1985 (31 March 1985 in the case of companies)**

$$\text{Allowance}^{(1)} = \text{Acquisition costs/31 March 1982 market value} \times \frac{RD - RI}{RI}$$

Where: RD = retail prices index for month in which disposal occurred; and

RI = retail prices index for either March 1982 or month in which acquisition occurred, whichever is the later.

**Note**

[1] Indexation allowance is restricted for disposals on or after 30 November 1993. The maximum allowance is limited to an amount equal to the unindexed gain and no allowance is available if there is an unindexed loss.

# Treatment of shares and other securities (after 5 April 1998)

(TCGA 1992, s. 106A)

Pooling for capital gains tax (but not corporation tax) ceased for acquisitions on or after 6 April 1998.

Disposals after 5 April 1998 are identified with acquisitions in the following order:

1. same day acquisitions[1] (under existing rule);
2. acquisitions within following 30 days;
3. previous acquisitions after 5 April 1998 on LIFO (Last-In-First-Out) basis;
4. any shares in 'pool' at 5 April 1998;
5. any shares held at 5 April 1982; and
6. any shares acquired before 6 April 1965.

If the above identification rules fail to exhaust the shares disposed of, they are identified with subsequent acquisitions.

**Note**

[1] Subject to election where shares acquired through employee share scheme on or after 6 April 2002 are disposed of after that date.

# Enterprise investment scheme

(TCGA 1992, s. 150A & Sch. 5B)

Under the enterprise investment scheme (EIS), income tax relief, CGT deferral relief and CGT disposal relief may be available and claimed. The income tax relief is based on the amount subscribed by a qualifying individual for eligible shares in a qualifying company. Income tax relief may be withdrawn under certain circumstances. With regards to the CGT reliefs:

(1) CGT Deferral Relief – Gains arising on the disposal of any asset can be deferred against subscriptions made by a qualifying individual for eligible shares in a qualifying company. For shares issued on or after 6 April 1998, shares no longer have to have EIS Income Tax Relief attributable to them in order to qualify for CGT Deferral Relief. The deferred gains may crystallise on the disposal of the shares.

(2) CGT Disposal Relief – Gains arising on the disposal by a qualifying individual of eligible shares in a qualifying company are exempt from CGT provided the shares have been held for a minimum period or the EIS Income Tax Relief has not been withdrawn.

'Qualifying individual' is basically someone who is not connected with the qualifying company.

'Eligible shares' are basically ordinary unquoted shares in a company.

'Qualifying company' is basically an unquoted company existing wholly for the purposes of carrying on a 'qualifying trade', or whose business consists entirely in the holding of shares in, or the making of loans to, one or more 'qualifying subsidiaries'.

'Qualifying trade' is basically one that is conducted on a commercial basis with a view to realising profits other than specifically excluded activities.

'Qualifying subsidiary' is basically one carrying on a qualifying trade.

## Charities

(TCGA 1992, s. 256(1))

The gains of charities are not taxable provided they are applicable, and applied, for charitable purposes only. Provisions contained in ICTA 1988, s. 505, 506 are designed to charge charities to tax on the amount of their income and gains that has not been invested, lent or spent in an approved way.

A charge to capital gains tax arises if a charity ceases to be a charity, when there is a deemed sale and reacquisition of the trust property by the trustees at market value.

## CGT exempt gilt-edged securites

The following list includes all gilt-edged securities (TCGA 1992, s. 288(8) and Sch. 9, para. 1) effectively designated as exempt, by TCGA 1992, Sch. 9, Pt. II. Any gains on such securities are not chargeable gains (TCGA 1992, s. 115(1)) and any losses are not allowable losses (TCGA 1992, s. 16(2)).

Securities may be added to the list in TCGA 1992, Sch. 9, Pt. II by Treasury Order. Orders made to date are:

* the *Capital Gains Tax (Gilt-Edged Securities) Order* 1993 (SI 1993/950);
* the *Capital Gains Tax (Gilt-Edged Securities) Order* 1994 (SI 1994/2656);
* the *Capital Gains Tax (Gilt-Edged Securities) Order* 1996 (SI 1996/1031);
* the *Capital Gains Tax (Gilt-Edged Securities) Order* 2001 (SI 2001/1122); and
* the *Capital Gains Tax (Gilt-Edged Securities) Order* 2002 (SI 2002/2849).

### Stocks and bonds charged on the National Loans Funds

| | |
|---|---|
| $2\frac{1}{2}\%$ | Annuities 1905 or after |
| $2\frac{3}{4}\%$ | Annuities 1905 or after |
| $2\frac{1}{2}\%$ | Consolidated Stock 1923 or after |
| $3\frac{1}{2}\%$ | War Loan 1952 or after |
| 4% | Consolidated Loan 1957 or after |
| $3\frac{1}{2}\%$ | Conversion Loan 1961 or after |
| 3% | Treasury Stock 1966 or after |
| $2\frac{1}{2}\%$ | Treasury Stock 1975 or after |
| $12\frac{3}{4}\%$ | Treasury Loan 1992 |
| 8% | Treasury Loan 1992 |
| 10% | Treasury Stock 1992 |
| 3% | Treasury Stock 1992 |

| | |
|---|---|
| $12\frac{1}{4}$% | Exchequer Stock 1992 |
| $13\frac{1}{2}$% | Exchequer Stock 1992 |
| $10\frac{1}{2}$% | Treasury Convertible Stock 1992 |
| 2% | Index-Linked Treasury Stock 1992 |
| $12\frac{1}{2}$% | Treasury Loan 1993 |
| 6% | Funding Loan 1993 |
| $13\frac{3}{4}$% | Treasury Loan 1993 |
| 10% | Treasury Loan 1993 |
| $8\frac{1}{4}$% | Treasury Stock 1993 |
| $14\frac{1}{2}$% | Treasury Loan 1994 |
| $12\frac{1}{2}$% | Exchequer Stock 1994 |
| 9% | Treasury Loan 1994 |
| 10% | Treasury Loan 1994 |
| $13\frac{1}{2}$% | Exchequer Stock 1994 |
| $8\frac{1}{2}$% | Treasury Stock 1994 |
| $8\frac{1}{2}$% | Treasury Stock 1994 'A' |
| 2% | Index-Linked Tresury Stock 1994 |
| 3% | Exchequer Gas Stock 1990–95 |
| 12% | Treasury Stock 1995 |
| $10\frac{1}{4}$% | Exchequer Stock 1995 |
| $12\frac{3}{4}$% | Treasury Loan 1995 |
| 9% | Treasury Loan 1992–96 |
| $15\frac{1}{4}$% | Treasury Loan 1996 |
| $13\frac{1}{4}$% | Exchequer Loan 1996 |
| 14% | Treasury Stock 1996 |
| 2% | Index-Linked Treasury Stock 1996 |
| 10% | Conversion Stock 1996 |
| 10% | Conversion Stock 1996 'A' |
| 10% | Conversion Stock 1996 'B' |
| $13\frac{1}{4}$% | Treasury Loan 1997 |
| $10\frac{1}{2}$% | Exchequer Stock 1997 |
| $8\frac{3}{4}$% | Treasury Loan 1997 |
| $8\frac{3}{4}$% | Treasury Loan 1997 'B' |
| $8\frac{3}{4}$% | Treasury Loan 1997 'C' |
| $8\frac{3}{4}$% | Treasury Loan 1997 'D' |
| $8\frac{3}{4}$% | Treasury Loan 1997 'E' |
| 15% | Exchequer Stock 1997 |
| 7% | Treasury Convertible Stock 1997 |
| $6\frac{3}{4}$% | Treasury Loan 1995–98 |
| $15\frac{1}{2}$% | Treasury Loan 1998 |
| 12% | Exchequer Stock 1998 |
| 12% | Exchequer Stock 1998 'A' |
| $9\frac{3}{4}$% | Exchequer Stock 1998 |
| $9\frac{3}{4}$% | Exchequer Stock 1998 'A' |
| $7\frac{1}{4}$% | Treasury Stock 1998 'A' |
| $7\frac{1}{4}$% | Treasury Stock 1998 'B' |
| 12% | Exchequer Stock 1998 'B' |
| $4\frac{5}{8}$% | Index-Linked Treasury Stock 1998 |
| $7\frac{1}{4}$% | Treasury Stock 1998 |
| $9\frac{1}{2}$% | Treasury Loan 1999 |
| $10\frac{1}{2}$% | Treasury Stock 1999 |
| $12\frac{1}{4}$% | Exchequer Stock 1999 |
| $12\frac{1}{4}$% | Exchequer Stock 1999 'A' |
| $12\frac{1}{4}$% | Exchequer Stock 1999 'B' |
| $2\frac{1}{2}$% | Index-Linked Treasury Convertible Stock 1999 |
| $10\frac{1}{4}$% | Conversion Stock 1999 |
| 6% | Treasury Stock 1999 |

| | |
|---|---|
| | Floating Rate Treasury Stock 1999 |
| 9% | Conversion Stock 2000 |
| 9% | Conversion Stock 2000 'A' |
| 9% | Conversion Stock 2000 'B' |
| 9% | Conversion Stock 2000 'C' |
| 8½% | Treasury Loan 2000 |
| 8% | Treasury Loan 2000 |
| 13% | Treasury Loan 2000 |
| 8% | Treasury Stock 2000 'A' |
| 13% | Treasury Stock 2000 'A' |
| 7% | Treasury Stock 2001 |
| 7% | Treasury Stock 2001 'A' |
| | Floating Rate Treasury Stock |
| 14% | Treasury Stock 1998–2001 |
| 2½% | Index-Linked Treasury Stock 2001 |
| 9¾% | Conversion Stock 2001 |
| 10% | Treasury Stock 2001 |
| 9½% | Conversion Loan 2001 |
| 10% | Treasury Stock 2001 'A' |
| 10% | Treasury Stock 2001 'B' |
| 12% | Exchequer Stock 1999–2002 |
| 12% | Exchequer Stock 1999–2002 'A' |
| 9½% | Conversion Stock 2002 |
| 10% | Conversion Stock 2002 |
| 9% | Exchequer Stock 2002 |
| 9¾% | Treasury Stock 2002 |
| 9¾% | Treasury Stock 2002 'A' |
| 9¾% | Treasury Stock 2002 'B' |
| 9¾% | Treasury Stock 2002 'C' |
| 7% | Treasury Stock 2002 |
| 13¾% | Treasury Stock 2000–2003 |
| 13¾% | Treasury Stock 2000–2003 'A' |
| 2½% | Index-Linked Treasury Stock 2003 |
| 9¾% | Conversino Loan 2003 |
| 8% | Treasury Stock 2003 |
| 8% | Treasury Stock 2003 'A' |
| 10% | Treasury Stock 2003 |
| 10% | Treasury Stock 2003 'A' |
| 10% | Treasury Stock 2003 'B' |
| 6½% | Treasury Stock 2003 |
| 3½% | Funding Stock 1999–2004 |
| 11½% | Treasury Stock 2001–2004 |
| 9½% | Conversion Stock 2004 |
| 10% | Treasury Stock 2004 |
| 6¾% | Treasury Stock 2004 |
| 6¾% | Treasury Stock 2004 'A' |
| 4⅜% | Index-Linked Treasury Stock 2004 |
| 9½% | Conversion Stock 2004 'A' |
| 5% | Treasury Stock 2004 |
| 12½% | Treasury Stock 2003–2005 |
| 12½% | Treasury Stock 2003–2005 'A' |
| 10½% | Exchequer Stock 2005 |
| 9½% | Conversion Stock 2005 |
| 9½% | Conversion Stock 2005 'A' |
| 8½% | Treasury Stock 2005 |
| 8% | Treasury Loan 2002–2006 |
| 8% | Treasury Loan 2002–2006 'A' |
| 2% | Index-Linked Treasury Stock 2006 |

| | |
|---|---|
| 9¾% | Conversion Stock 2006 |
| 7¾% | Treasury Stock 2006 |
| 7½% | Treasury Stock 2006 |
| 11¾% | Treasury Stock 2003–2007 |
| 11¾% | Treasury Stock 2003–2007 'A' |
| 8½% | Treasury Loan 2007 |
| 8½% | Treasury Loan 2007 'A' |
| 8½% | Treasury Loan 2007 'B' |
| 8½% | Treasury Loan 2007 'C' |
| 7¼% | Treasury Stock 2007 |
| 13½% | Treasury Stock 2004–2008 |
| 9% | Treasury Loan 2008 |
| 9% | Treasury Loan 2008 'A' |
| 9% | Treasury Loan 2008 'B' |
| 9% | Treasury Loan 2008 'C' |
| 9% | Treasury Loan 2008 'D' |
| 5% | Treasury Stock 2008 |
| 2½% | Index-Linked Treasury Stock 2009 |
| 8% | Treasury Stock 2009 |
| 8% | Treasury Stock 2009 'A' |
| 5¾% | Treasury Stock 2009 |
| 6¼% | Treasury Stock 2010 |
| 2½% | Index-Linked Treasury Stock 2011 |
| 9% | Conversion Loan 2011 |
| 9% | Conversion Loan 2011 'A' |
| 9% | Conversion Loan 2011 'B' |
| 9% | Conversion Loan 2011 'C' |
| 9% | Conversion Loan 2011 'D' |
| 5½% | Treasury Stock 2008–2012 |
| 5% | Treasury Stock 2012 |
| 9% | Treasury Stock 2012 |
| 9% | Treasury Stock 2012 'A' |
| 2½% | Index-Linked Treasury Stock 2013 |
| 8% | Treasury Stock 2013 |
| 7¾% | Treasury Loan 2012–2015 |
| 5% | Treasury Stock 2014 |
| 8% | Treasury Stock 2015 |
| 8% | Treasury Stock 2015 'A' |
| 2½% | Treasury Stock 1986–2016 |
| 2½% | Index-Linked Treasury Stock 2016 |
| 2½% | Index-Linked Treasury Stock 2016 'A' |
| 12% | Exchequer Stock 2013–2017 |
| 8¾% | Treasury Stock 2017 |
| 8¾% | Treasury Stock 2017 'A' |
| 2½% | Index-Linked Treasury Stock 2020 |
| 8% | Treasury Stock 2021 |
| 2½% | Index-Linked Treasury Stock 2024 |
| 5% | Treasury Stock 2025 |
| 6% | Treasury Stock 2028 |
| 4⅛% | Index-Linked Treasury Stock 2030 |
| 4½% | Treasury Stock 2032 |
| 2% | Index-Linked Treasury Stock 2035 |

## Securities issued by certain public corporations and guaranteed by the Treasury

| | |
|---|---|
| 3% | North of Scotland Electricity Stock 1989–92 |

104

# Expenses incurred by personal representatives
(SP 8/94)

In respect of deaths after 5 April 1993, the scale of expenses allowable in computing the gains or losses of personal representatives on the sale of assets in a deceased person's estate is as follows:

| Gross value of estate | Allowable expenditure |
| --- | --- |
| Up to £40,000 | 1.75% of probate value of assets sold by personal representatives |
| £40,001–£70,000 | £700, divided among all assets in the estate in proportion to their probate values and allowed in those proportions on assets sold by personal representatives |
| £70,001–£300,000 | 1% of probate value of assets sold |
| £300,001–£400,000 | £3,000, divided as above |
| £400,001–£750,000 | 0.75% of probate value of assets sold |
| Over £750,000 | Negotiated with the inspector |

**Note**

Computations based either on the above scale or on actual expenditure incurred are accepted.

# Time-limits for elections and claims

In the absence of any provision to the contrary, under self-assessment the normal rule is that claims are to be made within five years from 31 January next following the tax year to which they relate, otherwise the limit is six years from the end of the relevant chargeable period (TMA 1970, s. 43(1)).

For details of time-limits relating to payment of capital gains tax, see p. 51.

In certain cases the Board *may* permit an extension of the strict time-limit in relation to certain elections and claims.

| Provision | Time-limit | Statutory reference |
|---|---|---|
| Post-cessation expenses relieved against gains | 12 months from 31 January next following the tax year in which expenses paid | ICTA 1988, s. 109A |
| Trading losses relieved against gains | 12 months from 31 January next following the tax year loss arose | ICTA 1988, s. 380; FA 1991, s. 72 |
| Value of asset negligible | 2 years from end of tax year (or accounting period if a company) in which deemed disposal/reacquisition takes place | TCGA 1992, s. 24(2) |
| Re-basing of all assets to 31 March 1982 values | Within 12 months from 31 January next following the tax year of disposal (or 2 years from end of accounting period of disposal if a company) | TCGA 1992, s. 35(6) |
| 50% relief if deferred charge on gains before 31 March 1982 | Within 12 months from 31 January next following the tax year of disposal (or 2 years from end of accountancy period of disposal if a company) | TCGA 1992, s. 36 and Sch. 4, para. 9(1) |
| Variation within 2 years of death not to have CGT effect | 6 months from date of variation (election not necessary for variations on or after 1 August 2002) | TCGA 1992, s. 62(7) |
| Specifying which 'same day' share acquisitions (through employee share schemes) should be treated as disposed of first | Date of earliest disposal | TCGA 1992, s. 105A |

| Provision | Time-limit | Statutory reference |
|---|---|---|
| Replacement of business assets (roll-over relief) | 5 years from 31 January next following the tax year (or 6 years from the end of the accounting period if a company). Replacement asset to be purchased between 12 months before and 3 years after disposal of old asset | TCGA 1992, s. 152(1) |
| Disapplication of incorporation relief under TCGA 1992, s. 162 | 2 years from 31 January following the end of the year of assessment in which the business is transferred | TCGA 1992, s. 162A |
| Disposal of asset and re-investment in qualifying company (prior to 30 November 1993, applied only to disposal of qualifying shares or securities) (re-investment relief) | 5 years from 31 January next following the tax year (not available for acquisitions on or after 6 April 1998) | former TCGA 1992, s. 164A(2) |
| Hold-over of gain on gift of business asset | 5 years from 31 January next following the tax year | TCGA 1992, s. 165(1) |
| Determination of main residence | 2 years from acquisition of second property (see ESC D21) | TCGA 1992, s. 222(5) |
| Irrecoverable loan to a trader | 2 years from end of tax year (or accounting period if a company) otherwise effective from date claimed (see ESC D38, SP 8/90) | TCGA 1992, s. 253(3) |
| Retirement relief: ill-health grounds | 12 months from 31 January next following the year of assessment in which the disposal occurred | TCGA 1992, Sch. 6, para. 5(2) |

# INHERITANCE TAX

## Rates
(IHTA 1984, s. 7, Sch. 1)

| Gross cumulative total £ | Gross rate of tax % | Net cumulative total £ | Tax on each £ *over* net cumulative total for grossing up |
|---|---|---|---|
| **Lifetime transfers** | | | |
| **After 5 April 2004** | | | |
| 263,000 | Nil | 263,000 | ¼ |
| Over 263,000 | 20 | — | — |
| **6 April 2003–5 April 2004** | | | |
| 255,000 | Nil | 255,000 | ¼ |
| Over 255,000 | 20 | — | — |
| **6 April 2002–5 April 2003** | | | |
| 250,000 | Nil | 250,000 | ¼ |
| Over 250,000 | 20 | — | — |
| **6 April 2001–5 April 2002** | | | |
| 242,000 | Nil | 242,000 | ¼ |
| Over 242,000 | 20 | — | — |
| **6 April 2000–5 April 2001** | | | |
| 234,000 | Nil | 234,000 | ¼ |
| Over 234,000 | 20 | — | — |
| **6 April 1999–5 April 2000** | | | |
| 231,000 | Nil | 231,000 | ¼ |
| Over 231,000 | 20 | — | — |
| **6 April 1998–5 April 1999** | | | |
| 223,000 | Nil | 223,000 | ¼ |
| Over 223,000 | 20 | — | — |
| **6 April 1997–5 April 1998** | | | |
| 215,000 | Nil | 215,000 | ¼ |
| Over 215,000 | 20 | — | — |

| Gross cumulative total £ | Gross rate of tax % | Net cumulative total £ | Tax on each £ *over* net cumulative total for grossing up |
|---|---|---|---|
| **Transfers on death or within seven years before death** | | | |
| **After 5 April 2004** | | | |
| 263,000 | Nil | 263,000 | $\frac{2}{3}$ |
| Over 263,000 | 40 | — | — |
| **6 April 2003–5 April 2004** | | | |
| 255,000 | Nil | 255,000 | $\frac{2}{3}$ |
| Over 255,000 | 40 | — | — |
| **6 April 2002–5 April 2003** | | | |
| 250,000 | Nil | 250,000 | $\frac{2}{3}$ |
| Over 250,000 | 40 | — | — |
| **6 April 2001–5 April 2002** | | | |
| 242,000 | Nil | 242,000 | $\frac{2}{3}$ |
| Over 242,000 | 40 | — | — |
| **6 April 2000–5 April 2001** | | | |
| 234,000 | Nil | 234,000 | $\frac{2}{3}$ |
| Over 234,000 | 40 | — | — |
| **6 April 1999–5 April 2000** | | | |
| 231,000 | Nil | 231,000 | $\frac{2}{3}$ |
| Over 231,000 | 40 | — | — |
| **6 April 1998–5 April 1999** | | | |
| 223,000 | Nil | 223,000 | $\frac{2}{3}$ |
| Over 223,000 | 40 | — | — |
| **6 April 1997–5 April 1998** | | | |
| 215,000 | Nil | 215,000 | $\frac{2}{3}$ |
| Over 215,000 | 40 | — | — |

**Note**

The above scales apply to lifetime transfers made within seven years before death. For the tapered reduction in tax payable on transfers made between seven and three years before death, see following.

# Exemptions

### Annual and small gift exemption
(IHTA 1984, s. 19, 20)

|  | On or after 6 April 1981 £ |
|---|---|
| **Annual** | 3,000 |
| **Small gift** | 250 |

### Gifts in consideration of marriage
(IHTA 1984, s. 22)

| Identity of donor | Exemption limit £ |
|---|---|
| Parent of party to marriage | 5,000 |
| Remoter ancestor of party to marriage | 2,500 |
| Party to marriage | 2,500 |
| Any other person | 1,000 |

### Gift by UK-domiciled spouse to non UK-domiciled spouse
(IHTA 1984, s. 18)

| Transfer on or after | Exemption limit £ |
|---|---|
| 9 March 1982 | 55,000 |

# Agricultural and business property relief

| | Rate of relief for disposals | | | |
|---|---|---|---|---|
| Type of relief | Before 10/3/92 | 10/3/92– 31/8/95 | 1/9/95– 5/4/96 | On or after 6/4/96 |
| **Agricultural property** (IHTA 1984, s. 115ff.)[1] Vacant possession or right to obtain it within 12 months | % 50 | % 100 | % 100 | % 100 |
| Tenanted land with a vacant possession value | 50 | 100 | 100 | 100 |
| Entitled to 50% relief at 9 March 1981 and not since able to obtain vacant possession | 50 | 100 | 100 | 100 |
| Agricultural land let on or after 1 September 1995 | N/A | N/A | 100 | 100 |
| Other circumstances | 30 | 50 | 50 | 50 |
| **Business property** (IHTA 1984, s. 103ff.) *Nature of property* Business or interest in business | 50 | 100 | 100 | 100 |
| Controlling shareholding in quoted company | 50 | 50 | 50 | 50 |
| Controlling shareholding in unquoted[2] company | 50 | 100 | 100 | 100 |
| Settled property used in life tenant's business | 50/30[3] | 100/50[3] | 100/50[3] | 100/50[3] |
| Shareholding in unquoted[2] company: more than 25% interest | 50[4] | 100 | 100 | 100 |
| Minority shareholding in unquoted[2] company: 25% or less | 30[5] | 50 | 50 | 100 |
| Land, buildings, machinery or plant used by transferor's company or partnership | 30 | 50 | 50 | 50 |

**Notes**

[1] From 6 April 1995, short rotation coppice is regarded as agricultural property.

[2] With effect from 10 March 1992, 'unquoted' means shares not quoted on a recognised stock exchange and therefore includes shares dealt in on the Unlisted Securities Market (USM) or Alternative Investment Market (AIM).

[3] The higher rate applies if the settled property is transferred along with the business itself (*Fetherstonhaugh & Ors v IR Commrs* [1984] BTC 8,046).

[4] 30% if a minority interest transferred before 17 March 1987, or if transferor had not held at least 25% interest throughout preceding two years.

[5] The relief was 20% for transfers after 26 October 1977 but before 15 March 1983.

# Quick succession relief

(IHTA 1984, s. 141)

| Years between transfers | | Percentage applied to formula below |
|---|---|---|
| More than | Not more than | |
| 0 | 1 | 100 |
| 1 | 2 | 80 |
| 2 | 3 | 60 |
| 3 | 4 | 40 |
| 4 | 5 | 20 |

### Formula

$$\text{Tax charge on earlier transfer} \quad \times \quad \frac{\text{Increase in transferee's estate}}{\text{Diminution in transferor's estate}}$$

# Instalment option

(IHTA 1984, s. 227ff.)

*Interest-free*

- Controlling shareholdings
- Holdings of 10% or more of unquoted shares with value over £20,000
- Certain other death transfers of unquoted shares
- Business or interest in a business
- Agricultural value of agricultural property
- Woodlands

*Not interest-free*

- Land, wherever situated, other than within the categories above
- Shareholdings in certain land, investment and security dealing companies or market makers or discount houses

# Fall in value relief

| Type of property | Period after death |
|---|---|
| Quoted securities sold | One year |
| Qualifying investments cancelled or whose quotations suspended – deaths after 15 March 1992 | One year |
| Interests in land – deaths after 15 March 1990 | Four years |
| Interests in land – deaths before 16 March 1990 | Three years |

## Taper relief
(IHTA 1984, s. 7(4))

| Years between gift and death | | Percentage of full tax charge at death rates actually due |
|---|---|---|
| More than | Not more than | |
| 3 | 4 | 80 |
| 4 | 5 | 60 |
| 5 | 6 | 40 |
| 6 | 7 | 20 |

## Delivery of accounts
(IHTA 1984, s. 216)

| Transaction | Time limit |
|---|---|
| Chargeable lifetime transfer | Later of:<br>• 12 months after end of month in which transfer occurred<br>• 3 months after person became liable |
| Potentially exempt transfers which have become chargeable | 12 months after end of month in which death of transferor occurred |
| Transfers on death | Later of:<br>• 12 months after end of month in which death occurred<br>• 3 months after personal representatives first act or have reason to believe an account is required |
| Gifts subject to reservation included in donor's estate at death | 12 months after end of month in which death occurred |
| National heritage property | 6 months after end of month in which chargeable event occurred |

## Values below which no account required
(IHTA 1984, s. 256; SI 1981/880, 881, 1440 and 1441 as amended)

| Excepted lifetime chargeable transfers on and after 1 April 1981 | £ |
|---|---|
| Transfer in question, together with all other chargeable transfers in same 12-month period ending on 5 April | 10,000 |
| Transfer in question, together with all previous chargeable transfers during preceding ten years | 40,000 |

## Excepted estates (England, Wales and Northern Ireland only)

*Domiciled in the UK*

| Deaths on and after | But before | Total gross value[1] £ | Total gross value of property outside UK £ | Total value of settled property £ | Aggregate value of 'specified transfers' £ |
|---|---|---|---|---|---|
| 6 April 2002 | – | 220,000 | 75,000 | 100,000 | 100,000 |
| 6 April 2000 | 6 April 2002 | 210,000 | 50,000 | – | 75,000 |
| 6 April 1998 | 5 April 2000 | 180,000 | 30,000 | – | 50,000 |
| 6 April 1996 | 5 April 1998 | 180,000 | 30,000 | – | 50,000 |
| 6 April 1995 | 5 April 1996 | 145,000 | 15,000 | – | – |
| 1 April 1991 | 6 April 1995 | 125,000 | 15,000 | – | – |
| 1 April 1990 | 1 April 1991 | 115,000 | 15,000 | – | – |
| 1 April 1989 | 1 April 1990 | 100,000 | 15,000 | – | – |
| 1 April 1987 | 1 April 1989 | 70,000 | 10,000 | – | – |

**Note**

[1] For deaths on or after 6 April 2002 the limit of £220,000 applies to the aggregate of the gross value of the estate *plus* the value of specified transfers which is extended and includes chargeable transfers, within seven years prior to death, of cash, quoted shares or securities, **or an interest in land and furnishings and chattels disposed of at the same time to the same person** (excluding property transferred subject to a reservation or property which becomes settled property). For deaths on or after 6 April 1996 but before 6 April 2002 this limit applies to the total gross value of the estate *plus* the value of any transfers of cash or of quoted shares or securities made within seven years before death.

*Deceased never domiciled (or treated as domiciled) in the UK*

| Deaths on and after | Total gross value of estate in UK[1] £ |
|---|---|
| 6 April 2002 | 100,000 |

**Note**

[1] This must consist only of cash or quoted shares or securities passing by will, or under intestacy or survivorship in a beneficial joint tenancy, or by survivorship in Scotland.

# Penalties for failure in relation to obligations falling due after 26 July 1999

| Failure to deliver an IHT account (IHTA 1984, s. 216 | Account outstanding at end of statutory period | Up to £100 (but not exceeding tax due) |
|---|---|---|
| | Daily penalty after failure declared by a court or the Special Commissioners | Up to £60 a day |
| | Further penalty after six months from end of statutory period, if proceedings for declaring the failure not started before then | Up to £100 (but not exceeding tax due) |
| Failure by professional person to deliver a return of a settlement by a UK-domiciled person but with non-resident trustees (IHTA 1984, s. 218) | Account outstanding at end of statutory period (three months from making of settlement) | Up to £300 |
| | Daily penalty after failure declared by a court or the Special Commissioners | Up to £60 a day |
| Failure to comply with a notice requiring information (IHTA 1984, s. 219) | Penalty | Up to £300 |
| | Daily penalty after failure declared by a court or the Special Commissioners | Up to £60 a day |
| Failure to comply with a notice requiring documents, accounts or particulars (IHTA 1984, s. 219A) | Penalty | Up to £50 |
| | Daily penalty after failure declared by a court or the Special Commissioners | Up to £30 a day |
| Incorrect information provided by persons liable to tax (IHTA 1984, s. 247) | Fraud | Up to £3,000 plus the amount of the extra tax |
| | Negligence | Up to £1,500 plus the amount of the extra tax |
| Incorrect information provided by others (IHTA 1984, s. 247) | Fraud | Up to £3,000 |
| | Negligence | Up to £1,500 |
| Person assisting in providing incorrect information etc (IHTA 1984, s. 247) | Penalty | Up to £3,000 |

# Due dates for payment

(IHTA 1984, s. 226)

| Transfer | Due date |
|---|---|
| Chargeable lifetime transfers between 6 April and 30 September | 30 April in following year |
| Chargeable lifetime transfers between 1 October and 5 April | Six months after end of month in which transfer made |
| Potentially exempt transfers which become chargeable | Six months after end of month in which death occurred |
| Transfers on death; extra tax payable on chargeable lifetime transfers within seven years before death | Six months after end of month in which death occurred |

# Prescribed rates of interest

(IHTA 1984, s. 233)

| Period of application | Rate |
|---|---|
| From 6 November 2001 | 3 |
| 6 May 2001 to 5 November 2001 | 4 |
| 6 February 2000 to 5 May 2001 | 5 |
| 6 March 1999 to 5 February 2000 | 4 |
| 6 October 1994 to 5 March 1999 | 5 |
| 6 January 1994 to 5 October 1994 | 4 |

# STAMP DUTIES

## Conveyance or transfer on sale of shares and securities (FA 1999, Sch. 13, para. 3)

| Instrument | Rate of tax after 26 October 1986 % |
|---|---|
| Stock transfer | $\frac{1}{2}$[1][2] |
| Conversion of shares into depositary receipts | $1\frac{1}{2}$[3] |
| Take overs and mergers | $\frac{1}{2}$[1][2] |
| Purchase by company of own shares | [1][2] |
| Letters of allotment | $\frac{1}{2}$ |

**Notes**

[1] Because duty at $\frac{1}{2}$% is equivalent to £5 per £1,000 of consideration and duty is rounded up to the next multiple of £5 (FA 1999, s. 112(1)(b)), duty is effectively £5 per £1,000 (or part of £1,000) of consideration.

[2] Loan capital is generally exempt from transfer on sale duty subject to specific exclusions (designed to prevent exemption applying to quasi-equity securities) (FA 1986, s. 79).

[3] FA 1986, s. 67(3).

## Rates from 1 December 2003 (implementation of stamp duty land tax)

Transfers of property (consideration paid)

| Rate (%) | All land in the UK | |
|---|---|---|
| | **Residential** | **Non-residential** |
| Zero | £60,000 | £150,000 |
| 1 | Over £60,000–£250,000 | Over £150,000–£250,000 |
| 3 | Over £250,000–£500,000 | Over £250,000–£500,000 |
| 4 | Over £500,000 | Over £500,000 |

| Rate (%) | Land in disadvantaged areas | |
|---|---|---|
| | **Residential** | **Non-residential** |
| Zero | £150,000 | All |
| 1 | Over £150,000–£250,000 | |
| 3 | Over £250,000–£500,000 | |
| 4 | Over £500,000 | |

**Note**

[1] FA 2003, s. 125 confirms that property that is not land, shares or interests in partnerships is no longer subject to stamp duty from 1 December 2003.

# Conveyance or transfer on sale of other property (e.g. freehold property)

### Rates from 9 April 2003 to 30 November 2003

| Rate (%) | All property | Disadvantaged areas | |
|---|---|---|---|
| | | Residential | Non-residential |
| Zero | £0–60,000 | £0–150,000 | All |
| 1 | Over £60,000–£250,000 | Over £150,000–£250,000 | |
| 3 | Over £250,000–£500,000 | Over £250,000–£500,000 | |
| 4 | Over £500,000 | Over £500,000 | |

### Rates prior to 9 April 2003 (FA 1999, Sch.13, para. 4)

| Instruments executed | Thresholds | | | |
|---|---|---|---|---|
| | Up to £60,000 | Over £60,000 up to £250,000 | Over £250,000 up to £500,000 | Over £500,000 |
| On or after 28 March 2000[1] | Nil | 1% | 3% | 4% |
| On or after 16 March 1999[2] | Nil | 1% | 2.5% | 3.5% |

**Notes**

[1] Transfers executed on or after 28 March 2000 unless in pursuance of a contract made on or before 21 March 2000.

[2] Transfers executed on or after 16 March 1999 unless in pursuance of a contract made on or before 9 March 1999.

Stamp duty at the appropriate rate is charged on the *full* amount of the certified value, not just on any excess over a threshold. There is no duty on transfers listed in the table on p. 121.

## Fixed duties (FA 1999, s. 112(2))

In relation to instruments executed on or after 1 October 1999, the amount of fixed stamp duty is £5.

| Duty (pre-1/10/99) | Amount |
|---|---|
| Conveyance or transfer – miscellaneous | 50p |
| Declaration of trust | 50p |
| Duplicate or counterpart | 50p |
| Exchange or partition | 50p |
| Leases – small furnished letting | £1 |
| miscellaneous | £2 |
| Release or renunciation | 50p |
| Surrender | 50p |

**Note**

[1] FA 2003, s. 125 confirmed that property that is not land, shares or interests in partnerships is no longer subject to stamp duty from 1 December 2003.

## Leases (and agreements for leases) (FA 1999, Sch. 13, para. 11–13)

### Rates for instruments executed after 27 March 2000

| Term (FA 1999, Sch. 13, para. 12(3)) | Rate % |
|---|---|
| Under 7 years or indefinite:<br>• rent £5,000 or less<br>• over £5,000 | Nil<br>1 |
| Over 7 but not over 35 years | 2 |
| Over 35 but not over 100 years | 12 |
| Over 100 years | 24 |

**Notes**

[1] Leases for a definite term of less than one year: fixed duty of £5 (FA 1999, Sch. 13, para. 11 with effect from 1 October 1999).

[2] Where a furnished property lease is granted for a premium, this will be subject to stamp duty as set out in the table on p. 116 with the nil rate only applying if the annual rent does not exceed £600 per annum.

[3] An agreement for lease is liable to stamp duty as if it were an actual lease, but if a lease is subsequently granted which is in conformity with the agreement, or which relates to substantially the same property and term of years as the agreement, the duty on the lease is reduced by the duty already paid on the agreement.

## Duty on new leases from 1 December 2003

### Duty on rent[1]

| Rate (%) | Net present value of rent | |
|---|---|---|
| | Residential | Non-residential |
| Zero | £0–60,000 | £0–150,000 |
| 1 | Over £60,000 | Over £150,000 |

**Notes**

[1] These rates were introduced by FA 2003, s. 56 and Sch. 5.

[2] Duty on *premium* is the same as for transfers of land (except special rules apply for premium where rent exceeds £600 annually).

# Penalty for late presentation of documents for stamping

**Documents executed after 30 September 1999 (SA 1891, s. 15B)**

| Type of document | Penalties applicable if document presented for stamping more than |
|---|---|
| Document executed in UK | 30 days after execution |
| Document executed abroad relating to UK land and buildings | 30 days after execution (wef Royal assent to FA 2002) |
| Other document executed abroad | 30 days after document first received in UK[1] |

**Note**

[1] Free standing penalty (see table further below) may apply if written information confirming date of receipt in UK is incorrect.

The maximum penalties are:

- £300 or the amount of duty, whichever is less; on documents submitted up to one year late; and
- £300 or the amount of duty, whichever is greater; on documents submitted more than one year late.

# Mitigated penalties due on late stamping

The Stamp Office publishes tables (booklet SO10) of mitigated penalty levels that will be applied in straightforward cases.

**Cases involving ad valorem duties**

| Months late | Up to £300 | £300– £700 | £705– £1,350 | £1,355– £2,500 | £2,505– £5,000 | Over £5,000 |
|---|---|---|---|---|---|---|
| Under 3 | Nil | £20 | £40 | £60 | £80 | £100 |
| Under 6 | £20* | £40 | £60 | £80 | £100 | £150 |
| Under 9 | £40* | £60 | £80 | £100 | £150 | £200 |
| Under 12 | £60* | £80 | £100 | £150 | £200 | £300 |
| Under 15 | 15% of the duty or £100 if greater | | | | | See below |
| Under 18 | 25% of the duty or £150 if greater | | | | | |
| Under 21 | 35% of the duty or £200 if greater | | | | | |
| Under 24 | 45% of the duty or £250 if greater | | | | | |

**Note**

* Or the amount of the duty if that is less.

Cases over one year late involving duty over £5,000 and any case over two years late are considered individually.

**Cases involving fixed duties**

|  | Maximum penalty per document | Penalty after mitigation |
|---|---|---|
| **Up to 12 months late** | £5 | Nil (100% mitigation) |
| **Over 12 months late** | £300 | According to circumstances |

In all cases above the penalties will not apply if the person responsible for stamping can show a 'reasonable excuse' for the failure to submit the document(s) within the time limit. Interest is due on any unpaid penalty.

# Free standing penalties (maximum amount)

- fraud in relation to stamp duty; (£3,000)
- failure to set out true facts, relating to stamp duty liability, in a document; (£3,000)
- failure to stamp document within 30 days of issue of a Notice of Decision on Adjudication; (£300)
- failure to allow inspection of documents; (£300)
- registering or enrolling a chargeable document that is not duly stamped; (£300)
- circulating a blank transfer; (£300)
- issuing an unstamped foreign security. (£300)

# Duties abolished since March 1985

| Duty | Effective date of abolition |
|---|---|
| **Ad valorem** | |
| ● Capital duty | Transactions after 15 March 1988 – documents stamped after 21 March 1988 |
| ● Gifts inter vivos | Instruments executed after 18 March 1985, stamped after 25 March 1985 |
| ● Life assurance policy duty | Instruments executed after 31 December 1989 |
| ● Transfers on divorce etc. | Instruments executed after 25 March 1985 |
| ● Unit trust instrument duty | Instruments executed after 15 March 1988, stamped after 21 March 1988 |
| ● Variations and appropriations on death | Instruments executed after 25 March 1985 |
| ● Transfers of loan capital (subject to specific exclusions) generally (replaced previous provisions excepting certain categories of loan capital) | Instruments executed after 31 July 1986 |
| ● Duty on Northern Ireland bank notes etc. | 1 January 1992 |
| ● Transfers of intellectual property | Instruments executed after 27 March 2000 |
| ● Transfers to Registered Social Landlords | Instruments executed after 28 July 2000 |
| ● Stamp duty reserve tax on transfers of units or shares in collective investment schemes held in individual pension accounts (IPAs) | Transactions from 1 April 2001 |
| ● Transfers of land and leases in designated disadvantaged areas (for consideration/premium up to £150,000)[1] | Instruments executed after 29 November 2001 |
| ● Transfers of goodwill | Instruments executed after 22 April 2002 |
| ● Transfers of debts | tba (late 2003) |
| **Fixed duties** | |
| ● Agreement or contract made or entered into pursuant to the Highways Act. Appointment of a new trustee, and appointment in execution of a power of any property. Covenant. Deed of any kind whatsoever, not liable to other duties. Letter or power of attorney. Procuration. Revocation of any use or trust of any property by any writing, not being a will. Warrant of attorney. Letter of allotment and letter of renunciation. Scrip certificate, scrip. | Instruments executed after 25 March 1985 |
| ● Categories within the *Stamp Duty (Exempt Instruments) Regulations* 1987 (SI 1987/516): | Instruments executed after 30 April 1987 |
| A. Trust vesting instrument | |
| B. Transfer of bequeathed property to legatee | |
| C. Transfer of intestate property to person entitled | |
| D. Certain appropriations on death | |
| E. Transfer to beneficiary of entitlement to residue | |
| F. Certain transfers to beneficiaries entitled under settlements | |
| G. Certain transfers in consideration of marriage | |
| H. Transfers in connection with divorce | |
| I. Transfers by liquidator to shareholder | |
| J. Grant of easement for no consideration | |
| K. Grant of servitude for no consideration | |
| L. Conveyance as voluntary disposition for no consideration | |
| M. Variations on death | |
| N. Declaration of trust of life policy | Instruments executed after 30 September 1999 |

**Note**

[1] FA 2003, s. 125 confirmed that property that is not land, shares or interests in partnerships is not subject to stamp duty from 1 December 2003.

## Stamp duty reserve tax

Principal charge (FA 1986, s. 87)

| Subject matter of charge | Rate of tax % |
|---|---|
| Agreements to transfer chargeable securities[1] for money or money's worth | 0.5 |
| Renounceable letters of allotment | 0.5 |
| Shares converted into depositary receipts | 1.5 |
| *but* transfer of shares or securities on which stamp duty payable | 1 |
| Shares put into clearance system | 1.5 |
| *but* transfer of shares or securities on which stamp duty payable | 1 |

**Note**

[1] Chargeable securities = stocks, shares, loan capital, units under unit trust scheme (FA 1986, s. 99(3)).

## Interest on stamp duty and stamp duty reserve tax (SDRT)

In respect of instruments executed on or after 1 October 1999, interest is chargeable on stamp duty that is not paid within 30 days of execution of a stampable document, wherever execution takes place (*Stamp Act* 1891, s. 15A). Interest is payable on repayments of overpaid duty, calculated from the later of 30 days from the date of execution of the instrument, or lodgement with the Stamp Office of the duty repayable (FA 1999, s. 110). Interest is rounded down (if necessary) to the nearest multiple of £5. No interest is payable if that amount is under £25. The applicable interest rate is as prescribed under FA 1989, s. 178.

SDRT carries interest as follows:

- interest is charged on SDRT paid late (TMA 1970, s. 86 via SI 1986/1711, reg. 13);
- repayments of SDRT carry interest from the date that SDRT was paid (FA 1989, s. 178 via SI 1986/1711, reg. 11); and
- similarly, SDRT is repaid with interest if an instrument is duly stamped within six years of the date of the agreement (FA 1986, s. 92).

For interest periods from 1 October 1999 onwards, the rate of interest charged on underpaid or late paid stamp duty and SDRT exceeds that on repayments:

| Period of application | Rate % | |
|---|---|---|
| | Underpayments | Repayments |
| From 6 November 2001 | 6.50 | 2.50 |
| 6 May 2001 to 5 November 2001 | 7.50 | 3.50 |
| 6 February 2000 to 5 May 2001 | 8.50 | 4.00 |
| 1 October 1999 to 5 February 2000 | 7.50 | 3.00 |

# VALUE ADDED TAX

## Rates

| Period of application | Standard rate % | VAT fraction | Higher rate % | VAT fraction | Reduced rate %[1] | VAT fraction |
|---|---|---|---|---|---|---|
| From 1/4/94 | 17½ | $^7/_{47}$ | N/A | N/A | 5 | $^1/_{21}$ |
| 1/4/91–31/3/94 | 17½ | $^7/_{47}$ | N/A | N/A | N/A | N/A |
| 18/6/79–31/3/91 | 15 | $^3/_{23}$ | N/A | N/A | N/A | N/A |
| 12/4/76–17/6/79 | 8 | $^2/_{27}$ | 12½ | $^1/_9$ | N/A | N/A |
| 1/5/75–11/4/76 | 8 | $^2/_{27}$ | 25[2] | $^1/_5$ | N/A | N/A |

**Notes**

[1] Supplies of fuel and power for domestic, residential and charity non-business use and certain other supplies are charged at the reduced rate of 5% (VATA 1994, Sch. 7A).

[2] Re petrol, electrical appliances and luxury goods.

[3] Imports of certain works of art, antiques and collectors' items are charged at an effective rate of 5% from 27 July 1999 (2½% from 1 May 1995 to 26 July 1999).

## Registration limits

### Taxable supplies

| Period of application | Past turnover (£)[1] | | Future turnover (£)[1] |
|---|---|---|---|
| | 1 year | Unless turnover for next year will not exceed | 30 days[2] |
| From 10/4/03 | 56,000 | 54,000 | 56,000 |
| 25/4/02–9/4/03 | 55,000 | 53,000 | 55,000 |
| 1/4/01–24/4/02 | 54,000 | 52,000 | 54,000 |
| 1/4/2000–31/3/01 | 52,000 | 50,000 | 52,000 |
| 1/4/99–31/3/2000 | 51,000 | 49,000 | 51,000 |
| 1/4/98–31/3/99 | 50,000 | 48,000 | 50,000 |
| 1/12/97–31/3/98 | 49,000 | 47,000 | 49,000 |
| 27/11/96–30/11/97 | 48,000 | 46,000 | 48,000 |

**Notes**

[1] Value of taxable supplies at the zero rate and all positive rates are included.

[2] A person is liable to register if there are reasonable grounds for believing that the value of his taxable supplies in the period of 30 days then beginning will exceed this limit.

**Supplies from other member states – distance selling**

| Period of application | Cumulative relevant supplies from 1 January in year to any day in same year £ |
|---|---|
| From 1/1/93 | exceed 70,000 |

(VATA 1994, Sch. 2; Notice 700/1)

If certain goods subject to excise duty are removed to the UK, the person who removes the goods is liable to register in the UK because all such goods must be taxed in the country of destination. There is no de minimis limit.

**Acquisitions from other member states**

| Period of application | Cumulative relevant acquisitions from 1 January in year to any month in same year £ |
|---|---|
| From 10/4/03 | 56,000 |
| 25/4/02–9/4/03 | 55,000 |
| 1/4/01–24/4/02 | 54,000 |
| 1/4/2000–31/3/01 | 52,000 |
| 1/4/99–31/3/2000 | 51,000 |
| 1/4/98–31/3/99 | 50,000 |
| 1/1/98–31/3/98 | 49,000 |
| 1/1/97–31/12/97 | 48,000 |
| 1/1/96–31/12/96 | 47,000 |

**Assets supplied in the UK by overseas persons**

From 21 March 2000, any person without an establishment in the UK making or intending to make 'relevant' supplies must VAT register, regardless of the value of those supplies (VATA 1994, Sch. 3A). 'Relevant' supplies are taxable supplies of goods, including capital assets, in the UK where the supplier has recovered UK VAT under the eighth or thirteenth VAT directive. This applies where:

- the supplier (or his predecessor in business) was charged VAT on the purchase of the goods, or on anything incorporated in them, and has either claimed it back or intends to do so; or
- the VAT being claimed back was VAT paid on the import of goods into the UK.

# De-registration limits

**Taxable supplies**

| Period of application | Future turnover £ |
|---|---|
| From 10/4/03 | 54,000 |
| 25/4/02–9/4/03 | 53,000 |
| 1/4/01–24/4/02 | 52,000 |
| 1/4/2000–31/3/01 | 50,000 |
| 1/4/99–31/3/2000 | 49,000 |
| 1/4/98–31/3/99 | 48,000 |
| 1/12/97–31/3/98 | 47,000 |
| 27/11/96–30/11/97 | 46,000 |

Taxable supplies at both the zero rate and all positive rates are included in the above limits. However, the value of supplies of (1) 'capital assets' other than certain land supplies, (2) any taxable supplies which would not be taxable supplies apart from VATA 1994, s. 7(4), which concerns certain removals of goods to the UK, is excluded and (3) removals from a fiscal warehouse (VATA 1994, Sch. 1, para. 1 and 4; Notice 700/11).

**Supplies from other member states**

| Period of application | Past relevant supplies in last year to 31 December £ | Future relevant supplies in immediately following year £ |
|---|---|---|
| From 1/1/93 | 70,000 | 70,000 |

**Acquisitions from other member states**

| Period of application | Past relevant acquisitions in last year to 31 December £ | Future relevant acquisitions in immediately following year £ |
|---|---|---|
| From 10/4/03 | 56,000 | 56,000 |
| 25/4/02–9/4/03 | 55,000 | 55,000 |
| 1/4/01–24/4/02 | 54,000 | 54,000 |
| 1/4/2000–31/3/01 | 52,000 | 52,000 |
| 1/4/99–31/3/2000 | 51,000 | 51,000 |
| 1/4/98–31/3/99 | 50,000 | 50,000 |
| 1/1/98–31/3/98 | 49,000 | 49,000 |
| 1/1/97–31/12/97 | 48,000 | 48,000 |

# Special accounting limits

## Cash accounting: admission to the scheme

| Period of application | Annual turnover limit[1] £ |
|---|---|
| From 1/4/01 | 600,000 |
| 1/4/93–31/3/01 | 350,000 |
| 1/10/90–31/3/93 | 300,000 |

**Notes**

[1] Includes zero-rated supplies, but excludes any capital assets previously used in the business. Exempt supplies are also excluded.

[2] A person must withdraw from the cash accounting scheme at the end of a prescribed accounting period if the value of his taxable supplies in the one year ending at the end of the prescribed accounting period has exceeded (from 1 April 2001) £750,000 (*Value Added Tax Regulations* 1995 (SI 1995/2518), Pt. VIII; Notice 731).

## Annual accounting: admission to the scheme

| Period of application | Annual turnover limit £[1] |
|---|---|
| From 1/4/01 | 600,000 |
| 9/4/91–31/3/01 | 300,000 |

**Notes**

[1] Positive and zero-rated supplies excluding any supplies of capital assets and any exempt supplies.

[2] A person must withdraw from the annual accounting scheme at the end of a prescribed accounting period if the value of his taxable supplies in the one year ending at the end of the prescribed accounting period has exceeded (from 1 April 2001) £750,000 (*Value Added Tax Regulations* 1995 (SI 1995/2518), Pt. VII; Notice 732).

[3] Persons with a taxable turnover of up to (from 10 April 2003) £150,000 may join the annual accounting scheme immediately, i.e. without having to be registered for at least 12 months.

## Flat-rate scheme for small businesses: admission to the scheme

| Period of application | Annual taxable turnover limit[1] £ | Annual total turnover limit[2] £ |
|---|---|---|
| Returns ending after 9/4/03 | 150,000 | 187,500 |
| Returns ending after 25/4/02 | 100,000 | 125,000 |

**Notes**

[1] Zero-rated and positive-rated supplies excluding VAT. Exempt supplies are excluded.

[2] Total of VAT-exclusive taxable turnover and exempt and/or other non-taxable income.

[3] Net VAT liability is calculated by applying a flat-rate percentage to the VAT-inclusive turnover. The flat-rate percentage depends upon the trader sector (Notice 733). However from 1 January 2004, in the first year of VAT registration, the flat-rate percentage can be reduced by one per cent, i.e., if the normal rate is ten per cent, then nine per cent applies.

# Zero-rated supplies

(VATA 1994, Sch. 8)

| Group |
|---|
| 1. Food (this includes most food for human and animal consumption. The exceptions are mainly food supplied in the course of catering, confectionery, pet foods and hot take-away food) |
| 2. Sewerage services and water (except distilled and bottled water) but not if supplied to industry |
| 3. Books, pamphlets, newspapers, journals, maps, music etc. (but not stationery and posters) |
| 4. Talking books for the blind and handicapped and wireless sets for the blind |
| 5. Construction of buildings etc. |
| 6. Protected buildings |
| 7. International services |
| 8. Transport |
| 9. Caravans and houseboats |
| 10. Gold |
| 11. Bank notes |
| 12. Drugs, medicines, aids for the handicapped etc. |
| 13. Imports, exports etc. |
| 14. Tax-free shops (repealed for supplies made after 30 June 1999) |
| 15. Charities etc. |
| 16. Clothing and footwear |
| **Notes** |
| Except for exported goods and certain transactions in commodities, a supply is generally not zero-rated *unless* it is included in the zero-rated schedule (VATA 1994, Sch. 8). A supply which can be classified as zero-rated overrides exemption. A supply which is not outside the scope of VAT is standard-rated *unless* it falls within one of the categories of exempt or zero-rated or reduced-rated supplies. |

# Exempt supplies
(VATA 1994, Sch. 9)

| Group |
| --- |
| 1. Land |
| 2. Insurance |
| 3. Postal services |
| 4. Betting, gaming and lotteries |
| 5. Finance |
| 6. Education |
| 7. Health and welfare |
| 8. Burial and cremation |
| 9. Subscriptions to trade unions, professional bodies and other public interest bodies |
| 10. Sport, sports competitions and physical education |
| 11. Works of art etc. |
| 12. Fund-raising events by charities and other qualifying bodies |
| 13. Cultural services etc. |
| 14. Supplies of goods where input tax cannot be recovered (from 1 March 2000) |
| 15. Investment gold (from 1 January 2000) |
| **Notes** |
| The descriptions of the zero-rate and exempt groups are for ease of reference only and do *not* affect the interpretation of the groups (VATA 1994, s. 96(10)). Some suppliers can unilaterally elect to waive exemption of certain land and buildings (VATA 1994, Sch. 10, para. 2–4). |

# Reduced-rate supplies
(VATA 1994, Sch. 7A)

| Group |
| --- |
| 1. Domestic fuel or power |
| 2. Installation of energy-saving materials |
| 3. Grant-funded installation of heating equipment or security goods or connection of gas supply |
| 4. Women's sanitary products |
| 5. Children's car seats |
| 6. Residential conversions |
| 7. Residential renovations and alterations |

# Partial exemption

The partial exemption rules may restrict the amount of deductible input tax (*Value Added Tax Regulations* 1995 (SI 1995/2518), Pt. XIV; Notice 706).

Where input tax cannot be attributed directly to taxable or exempt supplies (residual input tax), the standard method apportions the residual input tax according to the values of taxable and exempt supplies made in a period. In relation to input tax incurred after 17 April 2002, persons must adjust the input tax deductible under the standard method at the end of their tax year if that amount is substantially different from an attribution based on the use of purchases. 'Substantially' means:

- £50,000 or greater; or
- 50% or more of the value of the residual input tax, but not less than £25,000.

Where the residual input tax is less than £50,000 per year, the standard method can be used, unless the person is defined as a group undertaking under the *Companies Act* 1985 and the residual input tax is greater than £25,000 per year.

De minimis limit for application of partial exemption rules is as follows:

| Period | Exempt input tax not exceeding |
| --- | --- |
| Tax years beginning after 30/11/94 | <ul><li>£625 per month on average; and</li><li>50% of total input tax for prescribed accounting period</li></ul> |
| Periods beginning between 1/4/92 and 30/11/94 | <ul><li>£600 per month on average</li></ul> |

# Capital goods scheme

(*Value Added Tax Regulations* 1995 (SI 1995/2518), Pt. XV; Notice 706/2).

From 1 April 1990 the capital goods scheme affects the acquisition, etc. by a partially exempt person for use in a business of certain items as follows:

| Item | Value | Adjustment period |
| --- | --- | --- |
| Computers and computer equipment | £50,000 or more | 5 years |
| Land and buildings[1] | £250,000 or more | 10 years (5 years where interest had less than 10 years to run on acquisition) |

Where the capital goods scheme applies, any initial deduction of input tax is made in the ordinary way, but must then be reviewed over the adjustment period by reference to the use of the asset concerned.

Revised rules apply to all capital goods scheme adjustments for intervals starting on or after 10 March 1999, to ensure that such adjustments compare the later use of the asset with the actual initial deduction of input VAT, after any other partial exemption adjustments.

**Note**

[1] From 3 July 1997, the capital goods scheme affects:

- civil engineering works; and
- the refurbishment or fitting out of a building by the owner.

# Particulars to be shown on a valid VAT invoice

(*Value Added Tax Regulations* 1995 (SI 1995/2518), Pt. III as amended).

### VAT invoices generally where supplied to a person who is also in the UK

| |
|---|
| 1. An identifying number |
| 2. The time of the supply |
| 3. The date of issue of the document |
| 4. The name, address and registration number of the supplier |
| 5. The name and address of the person to whom the goods or services are supplied |
| 6. Before 1 January 2004, the type of supply by reference to the following categories:<br>(a) A supply by sale<br>(b) A supply on hire purchase or any similar transaction<br>(c) A supply by loan<br>(d) A supply by way of exchange<br>(e) A supply on hire, lease or rental<br>(f) A supply of goods made from customer's materials<br>(g) A supply by sale on commission<br>(h) A supply on sale or return or similar terms, or<br>(i) Any other type of supply which the commissioners may at any time by notice specify |
| 7. A description sufficient to identify the goods or services supplied |
| 8. For each description, the quantity of the goods or the extent of the services, the rate of VAT and the amount payable, excluding VAT, expressed in any currency. Before 1 January 2004, the VAT-exclusive amount had to be expressed in sterling |
| 9. The gross total amount payable, excluding VAT, expressed in sterling |
| 10. The rate of any cash discount offered |
| 11. Before 1 January 2004, each rate of VAT chargeable and the amount of VAT chargeable, expressed in sterling, at each such rate |
| 12. The total amount of VAT chargeable, expressed in sterling |
| 13. From 1 January 2004, the unit price in relation to countable goods and services. However, the unit price may not need to be shown if it is not normally provided in a particular business sector and is not required by the customer |

Generally, until 31 December 2004 Customs should accept VAT invoices in the format required before 1 January 2004.

Persons providing VAT invoices for leasing certain motor cars must state on the invoice whether the car is a qualifying vehicle. This enables the lessee to claim the correct proportion of the VAT charged by the lessor.

The requirements for invoices concerning supplies intra-EU member states are in the *Value Added Tax Regulations* 1995 (SI 1995/2518), reg. 14(2).

## Retailers' invoices

If the supplier sells directly to the public, he is only required to issue a VAT invoice if the customer requests it. Furthermore, if the supply is for *£250* (before 1 January 2004, £100) or less, *including VAT*, a less-detailed VAT invoice can be issued setting out only the following:

| 1. The name, address and registration number of the retailer |
| --- |
| 2. The time of the supply |
| 3. A description sufficient to identify the goods or services supplied |
| 4. The total amount payable including VAT |
| 5. The rate of VAT in force at the time of the supply |

See Customs Notice 700 concerning the special rules for invoices concerning:

- petrol, derv, paraffin and heating oil;
- credit cards;
- another form of modified VAT invoice for retailers;
- cash and carry wholesalers;
- computer invoicing; and
- calculation of VAT on invoices.

## Continuous supplies of services

Certain additional particulars are required to be shown on a VAT invoice for a supply of continuous services, if the supplier chooses to use the advance invoicing facility (*Value Added Tax Regulations* 1995 (SI 1995/2518), reg. 90). Similar provisions apply for advance invoicing in respect of long leases (reg. 85) and in respect of supplies of water, gas, power, heat, refrigeration and ventilation (reg. 86).

# Reckonable dates

The reckonable dates for VAT are:

- *interest on overdue tax*: due date for submission of return (usually last day of month following end of return period);

- *interest on tax incorrectly repaid*: seven days after issue of instruction directing payment of amount incorrectly repaid.

Assessments of interest made after 30 September 1993 are restricted to the last three years (VATA 1994, s. 74(3)).

From 7 September 1994, Customs normally do not assess interest if it does not represent 'commercial restitution'.

From 1 February 1995, Customs normally do not assess interest on voluntary disclosures notified to Customs when the net underdeclaration is £2,000 or less. Customs' policy was already not to assess interest where a current-period adjustment is made.

From 6 July 1998, interest rates are varied (usually from the sixth day of a month) in accordance with a formula based on the average base lending rates of the main clearing banks (*Air Passenger Duty and Other Indirect Taxes (Interest Rate) Regulations* 1998 (SI 1998/1461)).

# Civil penalties, surcharge and interest

See above for reckonable dates.

| Provision | Current civil penalty etc. | |
|---|---|---|
| • VAT evasion<br>   conduct involving dishonesty[1] | Amount of VAT evaded or sought to be evaded, subject to mitigation (up to 100%) | |
| • Incorrect certificates as to zero-rating and reduced rate certificates re fuel and power, etc. | Customer is liable for any loss of tax with effect from 27 July 1999. VAT chargeable if certificate had been correct minus VAT actually charged. | |
| • Misdeclaration or neglect resulting in understatements or overclaims[1][2] | 15% of the VAT which would have been lost if the inaccuracy had not been discovered. | |
| • Repeated misdeclarations resulting in understatements or overclaims[1][3] | 15% of the VAT which would have been lost if the inaccuracy had not been discovered. | |
| • Failure to notify liability for registration or change in nature of supplies by person exempted from registration[1][4] | Period of failure | Percentage of relevant VAT |
| | 9 months or less | 5% |
| | Over 9, but not over 18 months | 10% |
| | Over 18 months | 15% |
| | (minimum penalty £50)<br>However, the relevant VAT is only calculated from 1 January 1996 rather than any earlier date if the liability to register followed a transfer of a business as a going concern. | |

| Provision | Current civil penalty etc. | |
|---|---|---|
| • Default interest (VATA 1994, s. 74) | For assessments calculated after 16 March 1993[5] interest does not commence from more than three years prior to the assessment date. However, interest continued to be charged until the related VAT is paid.[6] | |
| | From 6/12/03 | 6.5% |
| | 6/9/03–5/12/03 | 5.5% |
| | 6/11/01–5/9/03 | 6.5% |
| | 6/5/01–5/11/01 | 7.5% |
| | 6/2/2000–5/5/01 | 8.5% |
| | 6/3/99–5/2/2000 | 7.5% |
| | 6/1/99–5/3/99 | 8.5% |
| | 6/7/98–5/1/99 | 9.5% |
| | 6/2/96–5/7/98 | 6.25% |
| | 6/3/95–5/2/96 | 7% |
| | 6/10/94–5/3/95 | 6.25% |
| | 6/1/94–5/10/94 | 5.5% |
| • Default surcharge | 1st default in surcharge period | 2% |
| | 2nd | 5% |
| | 3rd | 10% |
| | 4th or later | 15% |
| | In the case of defaults occurring after 31 March 1992 but before 1 April 1993 the maximum surcharge rate was 20%; before 1 October 1993 a surcharge liability notice could be issued after a second default and the rate was 5% for a first default in a surcharge period, 10% for a second default, 15% for a third or later default. (£30 minimum. From 1 October 1993, if the taxpayer's return is late but no VAT is due, the surcharge is nil.) Customs generally only issue a surcharge assessment at the 2% or 5% rates for an amount of at least £200. A default surcharge can arise for persons who make monthly payments on account for return periods ending after 31 May 1996. | |

| Provision | Current civil penalty etc. | | |
|---|---|---|---|
| | For businesses with turnover of up to £100,000 (increase to £150,000 announced in Pre-Budget Report 2002 from April 2003) a penalty will only be levied after a written communication offering advice and help has been sent. | | |
| • Failure to comply with tribunal direction or summons | Up to £1,000 | | |
| • Unauthorised issue of VAT invoice[1] | 15% (30%: pre-1 November 1995) of the 'VAT' shown or amount attributable to VAT (minimum penalty £50) | | |
| • Breach of walking possession agreement | 50% of the VAT due or amount recoverable | | |
| • Breach of regulatory provision (Note: such a penalty cannot be imposed without a prior written warning (VATA 1994, s. 76(2))). | • Failure to preserve records: £500 | | |
| | • Submission of return or payment is late | | |
| | Number of relevant failures in 2 years before the failure | Greater of: | |
| | 0 | £5 or $\frac{1}{6}$ of 1% of VAT due | |
| | 1 | £10 or $\frac{1}{3}$ of 1% of VAT due | |
| | 2 or more | £15 or $\frac{1}{2}$ of 1% of VAT due | |
| | • Other breaches | | |
| | Number of relevant failures in 2 years before the failure | Prescribed daily rate £ | |
| | 0 | 5 | |
| | 1 | 10 | |
| | 2 or more | 15 | |
| | Penalty: the number of days of failure (100 maximum) multiplied by above prescribed daily rate (minimum penalty £50) | | |
| • Failure to submit EC sales statements[8] | 1st default including that to which the default notice relates | £5 per day | |
| | 2nd | £10 per day | |
| | 3rd | £15 per day | |

| Provision | Current civil penalty etc. |
|---|---|
| | (maximum: 100 days—minimum: £50) |
| • Inaccurate EC sales statements[8] | £100 for any material inaccuracy on a statement submitted within two years of a penalty notice (itself issued after a second materially inaccurate statement) |

| Provision | Current civil penalty etc. | |
|---|---|---|
| • Failure to notify acquisition of excise duty goods or new means of transport[1][4] | Period of failure | Percentage of relevant VAT |
| | 3 months or less | 5 |
| | Over 3 months but not over 6 months | 10 |
| | Over 6 months | 15 |

| Provision | Current civil penalty etc. |
|---|---|
| • Failure to comply with requirements of scheme for investment gold[1] | 17.5% of the value of the transaction concerned with effect from the passing of FA 2000 |
| • Failure by importers and exporters | Importers and exporters are subject to the civil evasion penalty for conduct taking place after 26 November 2003. A penalty can be imposed for non-compliance or evasion. Non-compliance includes:<br>1. occasional error involving at least £10,000 duty and/or import VAT;<br>2. persistent failure to comply with regulatory obligations; and<br>3. failure to correct deficiencies in systems, operations or physical security. |

**Notes**

[1] Mitigation may be available.

[2] For VAT prescribed accounting periods beginning after 30 November 1993 (although Customs normally applied the rules from 16 March 1993 (Customs News Release 32/93)) a penalty may be assessed if a return understates a person's liability by an amount which is at least the lower of:

• £1m; and

• 30% of the sum of output tax and input tax, the 'gross amount of tax'.

If a misdeclaration occurs as a result of the failure to draw the attention of Customs to an understated assessment, the reference above to the 'gross amount of tax' should be changed to the 'true amount of tax'.

[3] Repeated misdeclaration penalty may be assessed if:

• there are three or more misdeclared returns within 12 accounting periods;

• the misdeclaration in each period equals or exceeds the lesser of 10% of the 'gross amount of tax' (see[2]) and £500,000;

• Customs have issued a penalty liability notice; and

• at least two further misdeclarations occur during the eight periods completed following the issue of a penalty liability notice. This includes the period in which the notice is issued.

The above conditions apply to VAT prescribed accounting periods beginning after 30 November 1993, although Customs normally applied the rules from 16 March 1993 (Customs News Release 32/93).

[4] The rates given relate to original assessments made on or after 1 January 1995.

[5] Officially the capping of interest applies to interest on any assessment calculated on or after 1 October 1993, however Customs normally applied the new rules from 16 March 1993 when they were announced (Customs News Release 32/93).

[6] Customs generally do not charge interest where it does not represent commercial restitution (News Release 34/94, 7 September 1994).

(7) Intrastats (supplementary statistical declarations) – criminal offences:

- failure to submit declaration or to provide requested information – fine up to £2,500 (level 4 on the standard scale);
- a trader who knowingly or recklessly makes a false return, or falsifies a return, is:

(a) on summary conviction, liable to a fine up to £2,500 (level 4 on the standard scale) and/or three months imprisonment; and

(b) on indictment, liable to an unlimited fine and/or imprisonment up to two years.

(8) With effect from 27 July 1999 there is a two-year time-limit for assessing penalties relating to EC sales statements.

# Interest on overpaid VAT

Interest on overpaid VAT arises under VATA 1994, s. 78 in certain cases of official error:

| Period of application | Rate % |
|---|---|
| From 6 December 2003 | 3 |
| 6 September 2003 to 5 December 2003 | 2 |
| 6 November 2001 to 5 September 2003 | 3 |
| 6 May 2001 to 5 November 2001 | 4 |
| 6 February 2000 to 5 May 2001 | 5 |
| 6 March 1999 to 5 February 2000 | 4 |
| 6 January 1999 to 5 March 1999 | 5 |
| 1 April 1997 to 5 Janaury 1999 | 6 |
| 6 February 1993 to 31 March 1997 | 8 |

# Flat-rate scheme for farmers

(VATA 1994, s. 54)

| Period of application | Flat-rate addition % |
|---|---|
| From 1/1/93 | 4 |

## 'Blocked' input tax

Any input tax charged on the following items is 'blocked', i.e. non-recoverable:

- motor cars, other than certain motor cars acquired by certain persons but after 31 July 1995 (1) any person can recover input tax on motor cars used exclusively for business and (2) only 50 per cent of VAT on car leasing charges is recoverable if lessee makes any private use of the car and if lessor recovered the VAT on buying the car;
- entertainment, except of employees;
- in the case of claims by builders, articles of a kind not ordinarily installed by builders as fixtures in new houses;
- goods supplied under the second-hand scheme;
- goods imported for private purposes;
- non-business element of supplies to be used only partly for business purposes. This may contravene European law where the supplies are of goods: strictly the input tax is deductible, but output tax is due on non-business use. VAT on supplies not intended for business use does not rank as input tax, so cannot be recovered;
- goods and services acquired by a tour operator for re-supply as a designated travel service; and
- domestic accommodation for directors and their families to the extent of domestic purpose use.

In addition, 'exempt input tax' is not recoverable. From 10 March 1999, the partial exemption simplification rule that allowed some businesses to claim back all their input tax, providing that their exempt input tax is only incurred in relation to certain exempt supplies has been abolished.

## VAT on private fuel

(VATA 1994, s. 56)

For prescribed accounting periods *beginning* after 30 April 2003, the following table applies to assess output tax due on fuel used by cars for private journeys if it was provided at below cost from business resources. There is no high business mileage discount.

| | 12 months £ | VAT due per car £ | 3 months £ | VAT due per car £ | 1 month £ | VAT due per car £ |
|---|---|---|---|---|---|---|
| **Diesel** | | | | | | |
| *Cylinder capacity:* 2,000cc or less | 900 | 134.04 | 225 | 33.51 | 75 | 11.17 |
| over 2,000cc | 1,135 | 169.04 | 283 | 42.14 | 94 | 14.00 |
| **Petrol** | | | | | | |
| *Cylinder capacity:* 1,400cc or less | 950 | 141.48 | 237 | 35.29 | 79 | 11.76 |
| over 1,400cc up to 2,000cc | 1,200 | 178.72 | 300 | 44.68 | 100 | 14.89 |
| over 2,000cc | 1,770 | 263.61 | 442 | 65.82 | 147 | 21.89 |

For prescribed accounting periods *beginning* after 30 April 2002, but before 1 May 2003, the following table applies to assess output tax due on fuel used by cars for private journeys if it was provided at below cost from business resources. There is no high business mileage discount.

| From 1 May 2002 | 12 months £ | VAT due per car £ | 3 months £ | VAT due per car £ | 1 month £ | VAT due per car £ |
|---|---|---|---|---|---|---|
| **Diesel** | | | | | | |
| Cylinder capacity: 2,000cc or less | 850 | 126.59 | 212 | 31.57 | 70 | 10.42 |
| over 2,000cc | 1,075 | 160.10 | 268 | 39.91 | 89 | 13.25 |
| **Petrol** | | | | | | |
| Cylinder capacity: 1,400cc or less | 905 | 134.78 | 226 | 33.65 | 75 | 11.17 |
| over 1,400cc up to 2,000cc | 1,145 | 170.53 | 286 | 42.59 | 95 | 14.14 |
| over 2,000cc | 1,690 | 251.70 | 422 | 62.85 | 140 | 20.85 |

# VAT publications having legal force

The VAT publications that have legal force are listed in Notice 747.

# VAT registration numbers: country code prefixes

| Member state | Country code |
|---|---|
| Austria | AT |
| Belgium | BE |
| Cyprus[1] | CY |
| Czech Republic[1] | CZ |
| Denmark | DK |
| Estonia[1] | EE |
| Finland | FI |
| France | FR |
| Germany | DE |
| Greece | EL |
| Hungary[1] | HU |
| Ireland | IE |
| Italy | IT |
| Latvia[1] | LV |
| Lithuania[1] | LT |
| Luxembourg | LU |
| Malta[1] | MT |
| Netherlands | NL |
| Poland[1] | PL |
| Portugal | PT |
| Slovakia[1] | SK |
| Slovenia[1] | SV |
| Spain | ES |
| Sweden | SE |
| United Kingdom | GB |

**Note**

[1] This country is due to join the European Union in 2004.

# Customs National Advice Service (NAS)

Generally, the Customs National Advice Service (NAS) replaces the local business advice centres for certain purposes. Usually, it is available by telephoning 0845 010 9000 between the hours of 8am and 8pm Monday to Friday. The line tends to be less busy between the hours of 2pm and 4pm.

# INSURANCE PREMIUM TAX

## Rate

Imposed on certain insurance premiums where the risk is located in the UK (FA 1994, Pt. III).

| Period of application | Standard rate % | Higher rate % |
|---|---|---|
| From 1 July 1999 | 5 | 17.5 |
| 1 April 1997 to 30 June 1999 | 4 | 17.5 |
| 1 October 1994 to 31 March 1997 | 2.5 | n/a |

**Note**

From 1 August 1998, the higher rate applies to all travel insurance.

## Interest payable on certain asssessments

| Period of application | Rate % |
|---|---|
| From 6 November 2001 | 6.5 |
| 6 May 2001 to 5 November 2001 | 7.5 |
| 6 February 2000 to 5 May 2001 | 8.5 |
| 6 March 1999 to 5 February 2000 | 7.5 |
| 6 January 1999 to 5 March 1999 | 8.5 |
| 6 July 1998 to 5 January 1999 | 9.5 |
| 6 February 1996 to 5 July 1998 | 6.25 |
| 1 October 1994 to 5 February 1996 | 5.5 |

# LANDFILL TAX

Landfill tax was introduced on 1 October 1996 and is collected from landfill site operators (FA 1996, Pt. III).

Exemption applies to mining and quarrying waste, dredging waste, pet cemeteries and waste from the reclamation of contaminated land.

From 1 October 1999, exemption applies to inert waste used in restoring licensed landfill sites, including the progressive backfilling of active mineral workings.

| Type of waste | Rate (per tonne) £ |
|---|---|
| **Inactive waste** | 2 |
| **Active waste:** | |
| 1 April 2004 to 31 March 2005 | 15 |
| 1 April 2003 to 31 March 2004 | 14 |
| 1 April 2002 to 31 March 2003 | 13 |
| 1 April 2001 to 31 March 2002 | 12 |
| 1 April 2000 to 31 March 2001 | 11 |
| 1 April 1999 to 31 March 2000 | 10 |
| 1 October 1996 to 31 March 1999 | 7 |

## Interest payable on underdeclared landfill tax

(FA 1996, Sch. 5, para. 26)

| Period of application | Rate % |
|---|---|
| From 6 November 2001 | 6.5 |
| 5 May 2001 to 5 November 2001 | 7.5 |
| 6 February 2000 to 5 May 2001 | 8.5 |
| 6 March 1999 to 5 February 2000 | 7.5 |
| 6 January 1999 to 5 March 1999 | 8.5 |
| 6 July 1998 to 5 January 1999 | 9.5 |
| 1 April 1997 to 5 July 1998 | 6.25 |

### Environmental trusts

Site operators making payments to environmental trusts set up for approved environmental purposes can claim a tax credit up to 90 per cent of their contribution – subject to a maximum of 20 per cent of their landfill tax bill in a 12-month period. From 1 August 1999, operators using the scheme have up to an additional month every quarter to claim tax credits. On 15 October 1996, Customs approved an independent body, ENTRUST, as the regulator of environmental trusts. It is responsible for enrolling environmental bodies, maintaining their operation and ensuring that all expenditure complies with the landfill tax regulations.

# AGGREGATES LEVY

## Rate

| Period of application | Rate (per tonne) £ |
|---|---|
| From 1 April 2002 | 1.60 |

There is no registration threshold for aggregates levy. Any person who commercially exploits aggregate in the UK after 31 March 2002 may be liable to register with Customs and account for aggregates levy (FA 2001, Sch. 4 and the *Aggregates Levy (Registration and Miscellaneous Provisions) Regulations* 2001 (SI 2001/4027), reg. 2).

Generally, 'aggregate' means any rock, gravel or sand together with any other substances which are for the time being incorporated in or naturally occurring with it.

'Commercially exploited' generally means in the course or furtherance of a business the earliest of (FA 2001, s. 16):

- removal from:
    - the originating site;
    - a connected site that is registered under the same name as the originating site; or
    - a site where it had been intended to apply an exempt process to it, but this process was not applied;
- agreement to supply to another person;
- use for construction purchases; and
- mixing with any material or substance other than water, except in permitted circumstances.

# INDEX

*References are to page numbers*